The Hero Rises Up

'When he died he asked Hardy to kiss him: and he did. I think he would have asked anyone to kiss him – except his own wife.'

First staged at the Roundhouse, Chalk Farm, London, in 1968, this 'romantic melodrama' about Nelson, 'the last uncontested hero-figure of our own history', presents a vivid, ironic picture of some of the most famous and infamous exploits of Horatio Nelson prior to his elevation on a pillar in Trafalgar Square. Officially, a grateful nation applauded his unorthodox approach to the business of destroying enemy fleets and turned a blind eye to the unorthodoxies of his attitude to marriage. But the popular imagination was captured as much by the story of Nelson and Lady Hamilton as by that of his victories.

Here, making use of the style of popular print, legend and ballad, John Arden and Margaretta D'Arcy have brought the historical Nelson to life again and produced a pungent anatomy of a hero, of whom it is concluded: 'We needed him: he did what we required.'

The photograph on the front of the cover shows Henry Woolf and Bettina Jonic in a scene from the production at the Roundhouse and is reproduced by courtesy of Donald Cooper; the photograph on the back of the cover is reproduced by courtesy of David Naden Associates.

plays by John Arden and Margaretta D'Arcy

★

THE BUSINESS OF GOOD GOVERNMENT
THE ROYAL PARDON

plays by John Arden

★

SERJEANT MUSGRAVE'S DANCE
THE WATERS OF BABYLON
LIVE LIKE PIGS
THE HAPPY HAVEN
THE WORKHOUSE DONKEY
IRONHAND (adapted from Goethe's *Goetz von Berlichingen*)
LEFT-HANDED LIBERTY
ARMSTRONG'S LAST GOODNIGHT
SOLDIER, SOLDIER AND OTHER PLAYS

The Hero Rises Up

A Romantic Melodrama

by
JOHN ARDEN
&
MARGARETTA D'ARCY

METHUEN & CO LTD
11 NEW FETTER LANE · LONDON EC4

This Play is Dedicated to:
FRANK, the boy on the roof.

First published 1969
© *1969 by John Arden and Margaretta D'Arcy*
All rights reserved
Printed in Great Britain by
Cox & Wyman Ltd, London and Reading

An Asymmetrical Authors' Preface

When the Romans came to Britain, they came as a determinedly 'rectilinear' people of very *progressive* inclinations. Everything in this *conservative* 'curvilinear' island was to be IMPROVED: and the improvement (roads and so forth, for the movement of troops: chesters and so forth, for the accommodation of troops: offices and so forth, for the administration of troops ... always troops first, the local people second) was to be carried out with symmetry and efficiency, and, above all, *done properly*. The native Celts never entirely submitted. Then the Romans left us: and the English arrived. They found the military virtues of the Celts had been sufficiently smothered by the Romans and eventually they conquered these natives, despising them for their comparative lack of power, and – by extension – for their 'curvilinear' asymmetry. The Romans, whom they did not know first-hand, they did not despise. Indeed, with an inarticulate surly sense of inferiority and isolation, they admired and envied them: and when, at the time of St Augustine's Christian mission, the Romans came back again, the English received them with something like open arms – never an easy attitude for so churlish a people to adopt. The most important thing, it was generally agreed, should be to ensure that things were *done properly*. 'Muddling through' – as once in the Teutonic forests – was not to be permitted any more. Accounts were to balance: morality was to be consistent: and schoolboys who did not work out their sums but guessed the answer and got it right (as once in the Celtic glens) were straightway to be accused of looking up the solution on the back pages of their text-books and then beaten for taking liberties.

This play is about a man who was, by accident of birth and rearing, committed to a career governed by the old Roman 'rectilinear' principles. He himself was of asymmetrical 'curvilinear' temperament to an unusually passionate degree. But the English soon discovered how to handle him. He was *done properly*: wasted his extraordinary energy, courage, and humanity upon having men killed (in the end himself killed): and then finally was installed as a National Monument. We meant to write a play which need not be *done properly*. That is to say: we wanted to produce it ourselves, so that it would present the audience with an experience akin to that of running up in a crowded wet street on Saturday night against a drunken red-nosed man with a hump on his back dancing in a puddle, his arms around a pair of bright-eyed laughing girls, his mouth full of inexplicable loud noises. If you do see such a sight, what do you do? Nine times out of ten you push past among the wet mackintoshes and the umbrellas, muttering to yourself something about 'likely to get run over, ridiculous old fool – but why were those girls *laughing*?' and that's all. But you don't at once forget him: and although you know nothing about him and never will know anything about him, he has become some sort of *circumstance* in your life. You can't sit down and analyse him, because you haven't got the needful data: you can't ask him for his 'symbolism' – if he has any, you yourself will have provided it: and you can't go back and 're-evaluate' him, because the police will have moved him on. But there he was: and you saw him.

While we were producing the play we became involved in a quarrel with our management, the I CA. They had to *do things properly*, being responsible to their responsibilities (Roman, in a fashion; in a fashion originally intended for the administration of troops): and as the audience assembled we stood in the foyer like a pair of vexed Picts, committing what in my childhood was the prime social crime of the lower middle-class suburb where I lived – we were 'Brawling on the Doorstep' with the managerial representatives. Bewildered English persons, arriving to see the play, stood as Hengist and Horsa must once have stood at the ruined gates of decayed Londinium, touchingly inquiring – 'Can you please tell me – who is in charge here?' When we said we were the authors they did not regard that as an answer to their question. In the same way, a few weeks later, M. Godard, the film-director, stood helpless on the stage of the National Film Theatre asking people why they needed to see his latest film (about, among other things, the Black Revolution) when they could far more usefully send their money to the Eldridge Cleaver Defence Fund. So asymmetrical an approach, in his case, led to fisticuffs, and derision from the national press. We were a little luckier: we were able to shew the play in comparative peace: and later on we got a lawyer's letter. Things were, we supposed when we received it, *done properly* after all.

Which brings us back to what we regard as one of the most crucial and lastingly-significant decisions made in the whole of British history. After the Augustinian conversions in the south it was discovered that the northern English were already Christian and that they followed the Celtic rite, which – among other things – meant a different date for Easter. A conference was held between clergy of both factions, presided over by a king, in the hope of reconcilement. The Roman clerics said that they derived their authority from the Pope, who derived his from St Peter, who held the keys of heaven. The Celts could claim nothing save that they did what St Columba had always done, and *he* had been a very holy man. The king said, in effect: 'I cannot have two Easters. It is very discommodious, for when I am celebrating the feast with my men and getting extremely drunk, my queen, who is of the other persuasion, is keeping Lent in her apartments with her women, and abstaining from all carnal enjoyment. Therefore I decide that the Roman custom is the one we shall follow: because, holy though St Columba may have been, when I go to heaven I do not intend to find myself bandying words with the porter. I am not at all the sort of man to Brawl upon a Doorstep. It would be altogether most *improper*.' But – at least when the ephemeral art of the theatre is concerned – an art which depends upon nothing so much as an unpredictable and variable communication between living human beings – any rigid and unimaginative determination to *avoid* Doorstep-Brawling is only too liable to *set it afoot*.

So if the Theatre gets its money from Roman sources – i.e. any official body, with its inevitable subservience to a military requirement* – the asymmetrical 'curvilinear' *improper* practitioners of the art will either have to knuckle under or else fight so vehemently that the whole intuitive business of their lives will suffer radical distortion. This is a far subtler

*If this seems an extravagant generalization, just think of what happens to entertainment buildings, personnel and funds in the case of a military emergency. No doubt – in, say, 1940 – with full public support. But who tells the public when there is an emergency, and what measures they must take? Why was the start of World War I so irreversible? Because all over Europe the mobilization-plans, once under way, could not possibly be stopped. Why not? Because the various General Staffs all *said* they could not. Who has the last word? Caesar, Kaiser, Tsar – all the road-building, eagle-bearing, marble monsters of Imperium.

conflict than can be effectively analysed by setting up cliché-contrasts such as Censorship-against-Freedom. Often enough it is not even recognized as a conflict at all. The Theatre makes concessions and never admits to itself that it has done so. The Critics – who, as a body, seem not to understand upon how shifting a foundation their existence depends – will then write serious articles, deploring the failure of the dramatists or directors to keep in touch with the public. The public, by and large, like Lord Nelson, is inherently 'curvilinear' but under compulsion 'rectilinear': they will respect official art, but never love it. What they love they will love secretly and overtly despise, as did the first sour English when they ran up against the native Britons.

Secret love is marvellous but dangerous. As the fourteenth-century Welsh poet, Daffydd ap Gwilym, put it:

> 'Our love now is a pickpocket.
> He hoods his eyes and walks,
> One shoulder up, glancing,
> The corner of his mouth talks
> And no more than three words . . .
> Still he's dandy and courageous
> But with hard tactics in his head.
> He used to be a kind of a rambling bandit . . .
> On the crown of the road riding . . .
> But this was ridiculous.'

It involved him, do you see, in Brawls and Lawyer's Letters. But he was not deterred. He made a promise to his mistress:

> 'Nevertheless, after due interval,
> And with a more furtive proceeding,
> We shall continue our wantonness
> Through the seasons succeeding.'

And this, or something like it, appears to us to be the only hope for the future of our art. There is no way of being more specific. The times will bring to us their own appropriate strategies.

★

A practical note for directors and actors
There is no appropriate strategy for the presentation of this play. If you want to do it, you must do it how you like. But there are a few songs in the text which were written to fit extant airs and if they are not sung to those airs something of our dramatic intentions will be lost. They are:

Page 27   Song by EMMA and QUEEN: 'Most affronted King.'
           This is set to Handel's March from *Rinaldo* as quoted
           in *The Beggars' Opera* for the Highwaymen's Chorus
           'Let us take the road'.
Page 28   Song by EMMA and KING: 'Then with rage and with
           fear.' This is set to the well-known Anglo-Irish air
           'Lillibulero'.
Page 49   Song by PEOPLE: 'Join we great Nelson's name'.
           This is of course a new stanza for the National
           Anthem, and was composed by Emma's friend
           Cornelia Knight.
Page 50   Song by LADY NELSON: 'Through green fields and
           meadows'. This is a slightly adapted version of two
           stanzas from the folk-song 'All things are quite silent'
           which is published in *The Penguin Book of English
           Folk Songs* by Vaughan Williams and Lloyd.
Page 62   Song by HOST: 'He puts us all to shame'. This is best
           sung to the Irish air 'The rocky road to Dublin' as
           published in *Irish Street Ballads* by C. O'Lochlainn.
Page 68   Song by SEAMAN'S WIFE: 'Oh the weary cutters'.
           This is a song of Nelson's own period and may be
           found with its music in A. L. Lloyd's book, *Folk
           Song in England*.
Page 71   Song by NELSON, ALLEN and the ADMIRALS: 'And
           another one: Mrs Thompson'. This is set to the well-
           known shanty-air 'What shall we do with the drunken
           sailor'.
Page 84   Song by RELATIVES: 'There is nothing at all'. This
           is set to the eighteenth-century air 'Heart of Oak'.
Page 101   Song by NELSON and LADIES: 'The hero rises up'.
           This is set to the eighteenth-century air 'Rule
           Britannia'.
Page 101   Song by LADIES: 'With our hero now'. This is set to
           the eighteenth-century air 'Here's a health unto His
           Majesty' which can be fairly generally found.

There is no need for us to specify any particular sets for the
play, except that in the scene entitled 'You can't argue with a
Dead Man' (Page 39) some suggestion of under-water should
be provided. We did this by means of the Sensual Laboratory's
light-show: but there will be other methods. A paper screen
should ideally be provided for NELSON's first entrance: though
this can be dispensed with if convenient. The titles to each scene
ought not to be omitted. They can either be slide-projections or
painted placards and should remain throughout the scene that
they describe. The 'Necromantic Prologue' is optional.

                                                J. A. & M. D. A.

IMPORTANT PUBLIC NOTICE:
A NEW MELO-DRAMA!

At a Time when it appears well-nigh *impossible* that the Individual Human Being (however cowardly, indolent, gluttonous, concupiscent, idiotic or procrastinating he may be) should ever again assert his *potential* God-like Glory in the face of Established Financial Malice, the Merciless Use of the *Bludgeon* for the sake of Law-and-Order, and the Cold Concretion of Bureaucracy—

The **INSTITUTE** of **CONTEMPORARY ARTS**

(having, as is sadly admitted, certain unavoidable Connexions with the Bureaucracy aforesaid)

has determined to
EXPEND
a considerable sum of money

upon the presentation of a new Play, an apparent Lunacy on the part of this Institute which only the most *excessive* Public Support can prevent from causing the Immediate Ruin of the Administrators. For the Play—

THE HERO RISES UP

A Melo-drama by John Arden and Margaretta D'Arcy
concerns

The Life and Death of Vice-Admiral Lord Viscount NELSON. An *Individual* of many failings, but one who never paused to Think Twice: who never permitted his Sober Caution to *overrule* his Hot Resolve: who Did Not Care what the Timorous Critics of his age had to say in his *disfavour*.

Can Such a Man be Brought Complete upon the discredited Public Stage *today?* Can his Bold Career be *paid* for—in facsimile—by our putrescent blood-stained Modern Money? Should the ICA strike at its own roots to make this possible?

His *Own Hands* were stained an Honourable Scarlet!

❋   ❋   ❋

THE HERO RISES UP

contains *many* and *varied* Stage-spectacles of sensational splendour:

including—

(1) The Resurrection of the HERO NELSON from the *Dead*.

(2) The Republican revolt in *Naples:* and its shameful Repression by the Force of *British* Arms.

(3) The Strange and *Uncanny* Argument between the HERO and a *Dead Man*.

(4) A Drunken London *Orgy*, the curious behaviour of the HERO thereat: and his rejection of his *own* Wife in favour of LADY HAMILTON.

(5) The BLIND EYE at *Copenhagen*.

(6) The *unconventional* Domesticity of LADY HAMILTON with what amounted to *Two* Husbands beneath *One* Roof.

(7) TRAFALGAR: Glory: Grief: Despair: & Exultation!!

(8) The HERO *ascends* into His *Fitting* Paradise.

———— ❀ ❀ ❀ ————

DO NOT FAIL to attend this Momentous Celebration of the Historic Grandeur of our Island Race: **DO NOT FAIL** to see What Once We Were: **DO NOT FAIL** to make the Dismal Comparison with What We Are Now!!

THE HERO RISES UP

The Hero Rises Up was first presented by the Institute of Contemporary Arts at the Round House, Chalk Farm, on November 6th 1968 with the cast shewn below:

LORD NELSON	Henry Woolf
NISBET (*His stepson*)	David Leland
HAMILTON (*British Ambassador at Naples*)	
CARACCIOLO (*Neapolitan Minister of Marine*)	John Preston
HARDY (*Captain R.N.*)	
ALLEN (*Nelson's Sailor-servant*)	Robert Gillespie
KING OF NAPLES	
A PRINCE (*of the House of Hanover*)	
ST VINCENT (*Admiral R.N.*)	John Rye
A CLERGYMAN (*of St Paul's*)	
CARDINAL OF CALABRIA	
KEITH (*Admiral R.N.*)	
HOST (*at a Party in London*)	Wilfrid Downing
PARKER (*Admiral R.N.*)	
Other Male Parts were played by	Robert Reiser
2 GENERAL UTILITY GENTLEMEN	Arthur Holden
EMMA, (*Lady Hamilton*)	Bettina Jonic
QUEEN OF NAPLES	
LADY NELSON	Ann Mitchell
MRS CADOGAN (*Emma's Mother*)	Anna Wing
A DOLLY	
A SEAMAN'S WIFE	Jennie Short
A MERMAID	
A DOLLY	
A MERMAID	Mary Rutherford

Crowds, Sailors, etc., were played by members of the Havering Youth Theatre Workshop.

Music by Boris Howarth

Décor and Costumes by Margaret Hogg, Ted Parker and Jeanne Jones

Light-show by The Sensual Laboratory.

*

N.B. The Play can be presented with only Seven Gentlemen and Four Ladies, which means there should be one DOLLY (as in the text), one MERMAID and one GENERAL UTILITY GENTLEMAN.

*

The Hero Rises Up

A Necromantic Prologue

(to be spoken by an Academic Representative of the Authors)

To what extent the history of the human race is determined
by the abstract and indeed scarcely tangible, though none the
less mensurable, forces of economics, population-growth,
routes of communication, geographical barriers and the
absence of geographical barriers, pastoral and/or agricultural
and/or industrial systems of production – and similar kindred
phenomena – must at the present time be regarded as subject
to controversy. No less controversial is the importance we
should accord the individual human being in such a universal
schema – what Professor Krankenschwester of Leipzig has
called the Upthrust or 'Hüpfauf' of the single unit in the
midst of the undifferentiated mass. Krankenschwester's great
work on this subject is of course his three-volume opus '*Die
Merkwürdige Heldenbahn*' or 'What makes a man a Hero' – to
translate the title into somewhat demotic terms. Krankenschwester provides no clear answer: the fact that his book
was published in April 1945 suggests that his research was
having to be continually modified to keep pace with the devel-
opment of public events in Germany at that time: and con-
ceivably a certain internal confusion within the author's mind
allowed itself to be transferred to the pages of his final chapters.
But be that as it may: the Krankenschwester theory received
startling confirmation in the post-war works of the French
savant Vespasien Ladrogue who – in a short but pungent
study entitled '*Le Sang et La Merde de la Guerre*' established
once and for all that the great commanders of history – in this
case of course French history – were in fact responsible not
only for winning battles but also for losing them. Ladrogue
refers frequently to the neglected but seminal Scottish philo-

sopher, the Reverend Hosea Farquharson, who, as long ago
as 1864, in an unpublished sermon on the conflict between
David and Goliath, demonstrated conclusively that in any
form of human combat one man and one man only may be
shewn to be in direct receipt of supernatural guidance – what
Farquharson calls 'The Hand of the Lord of Hosts' – and
thus may be presumed to be inevitably destined to win. The
allocation of this helpful assistance from an extra-terrestrial
source does not seem to be dictated by any particular qualities
or lack of qualities in one or other cause for which the combat
is being fought. In other words: an heroic leader might just
as well be on the other side from oneself: this does not diminish his greatness: nor does it mean that one's own cause is
necessarily ignoble. It merely serves to shew that God has
decided – in what Dr Farquharson calls 'His Infinite Wisdom'
– that victory is to be allotted to the enemy – at least for the
time being. This is a very severe Calvinist view and I am not
entirely able to accept it. But what one must, I think, accept,
is the impossibility of determining, except by means of hind-
sight, exactly who the hero – in any given situation – is. As
Ladrogue puts it – '*Le Conquérant, c'est lui*' – you cannot
predict a hero, however badly you need one: unless – and here
we come to the main purpose of our meeting here tonight –
unless hitherto untapped areas of research are to be brought
under examination. We live today, it is generally recognized,
in an age of despair: and the search for a truly heroic, god-like
figure to lead us out of our trials and tribulations, is common
to us all. Even in the regrettable realms of radical-syndicalist-
insurrectionary leftism there are the potent mythical figures
of Che Guevara and Mao Tse Tung and – and so on and so
forth. To understand what makes a hero is to understand,
perhaps, how we in our own society may be able to make one
for ourselves – or even become one – who knows? Let us
consider the last uncontested hero-figure of our own history –
Lord Nelson. A man beloved, successful, and abundantly
commemorated both by the established ruling circles and the
undifferentiated popular sludge. I propose to do no less than
resurrect his spirit. And also to resurrect the spirit of the

woman whom he regarded as 'His Guardian Angel' – an intermediary, as it were, between the hero himself and Dr Farquharson's 'Lord of Hosts', his inspiratrix, his muse of battle, his – his notorious concubine. The technique I shall employ for this necromantic experiment does not involve catch-penny invocations and incantations: which are nowadays completely discredited. No: all I need is this simple electro-static apparatus – here – combined with your absolute concentration and co-operation. When Lord Nelson and his woman are summoned before us, I want you all to observe them, what they do, and what they say: and to learn from it such lessons for your future as you may. *That* is the part of the proceedings in which I have no competence to guide you. If you are wise, you will benefit: if you are foolish, you will not. But first, I must have complete silence: and I want you to meditate, as pungently as you can, upon the sexual congress of Lord Nelson and Lady Hamilton. This act, which, we have reason to believe, they did not perform infrequently, was naturally the nearest approach, one to the other, which they were able to make during their lives upon this earth. So think about it – think about it very deeply, consider it in all its manifold vibrations, complexities, and alternations of posture. I want to hear you all breathing very hard indeed . . .

The lights are lowered until only the glow of the 'apparatus' and the light behind the screen remain.
NELSON's *shadow appears upon the screen.*

Act One

NELSON *bursts through the screen – he wears a patch over one eye, and one sleeve sewn up over his missing arm.*

NELSON. If you don't know who I am you ought to be ashamed of yourselves, God damn your eyes. You are, I take it, Englishmen? Is there any point in my informing you of all the great deeds I have done for you? My victories? St Vincent, the Nile, Copenhagen, Trafalgar? Of the techniques by which I achieved them? Surely all such history is already sufficiently known. I was the first naval commander who understood – and put into practice – the theory of the entire and total destruction of the enemy fleet, at whatever cost to my own. A destruction made possible by my enthusiastic disregard of everybody's orders – the orders of my immediate superiors, and also the unwritten but potent orders provided by two hundred years of conservative naval tradition. I marvel that you do not – at this point – throw your hats into the air and cheer. It is customary to do so. No matter – I have had my reward:

(*He sings.*)

> They set me on a pillar
> At the north end of Whitehall,
> For every inch of that great pillar
> A Frenchman I did kill.
>
> Like a carronade my one good eye
> I level at Westminster:
> Neither with pride nor patronage
> But a black and bitter cheer.

And why?

I broke the rules of warfare
And the nation did forgive:
But there was no forgiveness when
I broke the rules of love.

Lady Hamilton was my one true love. I left her to this
nation in my last will and testament and King George and
his Ministers would not honour the bequest.

(*He sings.*)

For to me the English people
Or the people of any land
Are incarnate in the crowned head
Of the King upon his throne.

For is not that why the war was fought?
When the crownèd head of France
In the reeking bloody basket had
Been forced to leap and dance.

And in the end of course the French realized that without
their King they were nowhere: so they had to construct
one. But you can't do that – royalty is not to be put on and
taken off like a topman's tarpaulin coat. In any case their
great Napoleon was entirely inadequate: and I was the
first one to prove it before all the world – he met his match
when he met me:

(*He sings.*)

Bonaparte was a soldier
Who never went on the sea:
But he ordered out his sailormen
To win him victory.

For liberty equality
Fraternity, he would cry
All Frenchmen must become my slaves
And for my glory die.

And die they did indeed: and he himself I could have

killed. The greatest failure of my career. Shortly before the
Battle of the Nile he and all his generals and all the soldiers
of his Army were at sea in undefended transport-ships
within a league of my own fleet: but it was at night in thick
fog, and I miscalculated and I missed them.

> He was nothing more than two bright eyes
> Glowing in the dark:
> He was nothing more than a sullen muttering
> Round the corner of my work.
> I did not see him: and his name
> Was one at that time I had never heard –
> How could I know that I kept alive
> The worst man in the world?

He sinks down in dejection.

THE HEROINE UTTERS HER DEFIANCE:

EMMA *enters.*

EMMA. Nelson: rise up! You are not here to repine for what
no man could have been expected to achieve. Bonaparte
you did not kill, but the whole French fleet of line-of-battle-
ships a few days later in Aboukir Bay you burnt and sank
and blew into ludicrous fragments.
NELSON. My dearest Emma, my Guardian Angel, the mother
of my child, I am not well.
EMMA. You are seasick.
NELSON. I am always seasick.
EMMA. You are seasick and you are lovesick.
NELSON. I lived with you for years and on my death you
were forgotten. I have come here to complain about it,
God damn it.
EMMA. You are swearing again. And you will never convince
anyone by huddling yourself up in a tight little bundle of
hysterical self-pity.
NELSON. What? You are Emma? You are my Lady Hamilton?
Oh you have her appearance rightly enough –

Tall and broad and in full sail
You are my Emma to the life:
Why then do you have to talk
In the voice of my wife?

EMMA. I am your wife!

NELSON. But, Fanny was my wife.

EMMA. You were married to Fanny. But you did not love
her –

NELSON. I esteemed her –

EMMA. Yes: but far more than that is involved and should be
stated: bold and brazen:

(*She sings.*)

To be married to a man
It is not enough to stand
With your fingers a-touching at his fingers' ends
Or even hand-in-hand.

It is not enough to lie
Among the grass and flowers
Or deep in the waves of a wide and moonlit bed
Ride out the floodtide hours.

All this I have enjoyed
So many and many a time
So many a young man I have swallowed up alive
And believed that he was mine.

Lord Nelson is not young
Although he is very small:
I enfolded my flesh round his skinny little ribs
But he nailed me to the wall.

CAPTAIN NISBET'S DISSENT:

Enter NISBET (*in his uniform*).

NISBET. No no no! A wife is a wife and his wife was my
mother. I am not going to permit them to shovel her under
the orlop deck. Nor the other one, either.

NELSON. What other one?

NISBET. The British Ambassador in Naples – Sir William
Hamilton, no less.

EMMA. Why – you young hobbledehoy –

NELSON. My dear, he *is* my stepson. We ought not to be dis-
courteous. And for that matter, Josiah, neither ought you.

EMMA. Very well then: Josiah: Captain Josiah Nisbet, Royal
Navy – do not you dare to speak to me of Sir William
Hamilton, my good husband – you are not able to com-
prehend a relationship of such affection and true delicacy
as obtained between him and *us*!

NISBET. If I am not able, perhaps there are others who are.
So elucidate it, why don't you? Explain it from the begin-
ning. With all its attendant circumstances.

NELSON. Let us do so.
> We should not scorn
> The callow fury of this young man.
> Let him bite – as he has always bittten –
> Into the heart of my glory
> And the gut of my reputation:
> We can render him, in good measure,
> And with no prevarication,
> Our clear and unremorseful story
> Of what happened, when, and why.

NISBET. So make sure that you tell the truth. And do not
compel me to correct you.

(*He sings.*)

> I was there and I saw it, the start of your story
> Was not at any moment of victory and joy:
> But a time of confusion and bloody-minded treason
> When the honour of Old England had wilted away.

NELSON. My God, he means the business about –

EMMA. Why damn him, he means the business –

NISBET. Ho yes, he means the business of –

ALL THREE. Commodore Caracciolo!

NISBET. Oho, do you see that their faces are quite pale? It

has taken full six inches off her majestical height and his own little cock-sparrow head is sunk deep into his shoulder.

(*He sings.*)

> For what deed is it possible
> That they can feel ashamed ?
> Whatever did they do
> That I can hold them to blame ?
>
> It cannot be the kissing
> And tossing and poking
> Of flesh that was already
> By another one bespoken.

They have demonstrated well enough that that made them nothing but *proud*. So let us place it. After the Battle of the Nile, Naples was technically neutral. King Ferdinand was the abominable monarch . . .

Enter the KING.

Lord Nelson persuaded him to commit himself against the French. But the French forthwith defeated him. His people rose for –
A CRY. Liberty. A Republic. Death to the Bourbon tyrants.

The KING *wilts. He then starts to run around the stage. The other characters join him as* NISBET *names them,* EMMA *bringing up the rear: and* NELSON *places himself at the head of the chain.*

NISBET. So King Ferdinand, being abominable, fled. With his Queen. And Sir William Hamilton. And Sir William's wife's mother. And Admiral Nelson, in a British line-of-battle-ship, brought them all to – Palermo.

The chain of fleeing personages halts: and they take their places for the next scene.

TO PALERMO COMES A MESSAGE:

EMMA. At this time I had not declined
          From the bed of my good man.
HAMILTON. Not that there was anything in that bed I could
          do.
          Old age and rheumatism in back and in hand
          Rendered me fit for little good where the ladies were
          concerned.
          But as usual I turned
          To the agreeable activity
          Of collecting and arranging such articles of antiquity
          As the Greeks, Romans and Carthaginians had been
          so kind
          Both in Naples and Sicily to fabricate and leave behind:
          Statues, vases, carvings, easy enough to find:
          And having found them, I sit amongst them, and take
          my quiet pleasure
          From their impeccable proportions. Such delight it is
          to measure
          The thews and sinews of a Hercules, even when in
          miniature . . .

He is rapt in the study of a bronze statuette. EMMA *yawns and stretches.* MRS CADOGAN *checks her with a gesture, pointing to the* KING *and* QUEEN, *who are sitting bolt upright in a very formal posture.* NELSON *paces irritably about at a little distance.*

EMMA (*sings, quietly*).

          Oh weary the long ninth wave
          That breaks upon the stony strand:
          And weary the heart of the exile
          So far from his native land.

A DOLLY *runs in excitedly and jumps at* NELSON, *kissing him with some violence, and laughing at his surprise. He puts his finger to her lips and leads her dexterously away from the others. They commence to roll and tumble together.*

NISBET. A married man at home is a bachelor at sea. He was always a very venereal kind of fellow. Oh I've done it myself of course with the same class of young woman, and it would be foolish to feel resentment. I am sure my mother would understand perfectly.

Enter ALLEN.

ALLEN. Not but what in his case it did tend to run to extremes. Two at a time sometimes and frequently on board ship at quite disastrous crises of naval activity –

(*He sings.*)

> Of a morning, in his cabin
> Oh in port or out at sea,
> I'd go in to swab his deck-boards
> In his bunk there she would be.
>
> She'd stretch her arms and give a yawn
> And stick her toes from out the sheet
> Sometimes black and sometimes yeller
> Fat or thin but always sweet.
>
> Little whores from old Livorno
> Green-eyed Jenny from Genoa town
> Red-haired Rosa from Gibraltar
> Whatever she were, he'd lay her down.
>
> We had a sweepstake on the gun-deck
> Would the next one be mucky or clean?
> And he always said the same to me,
> When he knew what I had seen –

NELSON. Goddammit, Allen, you disgusting filthy beast –
ALLEN. Yerss – that was it . . . Did you call me, sir?
NELSON. No I didn't: but now that you're here, you might as well do some work. Shew the young lady out.
ALLEN. Aye aye, sir . . . This way, ma'am, if you please.

She gives NELSON *a farewell kiss, and he gives her some money, and* ALLEN *escorts her out and then returns.*

NELSON (*as she leaves*). I am sorry my dismissal must be so abrupt, my sweetheart, but the news you have brought me craves an immediate return to duty. Allen, are you back yet? I said duty: I'm not dressed for it!

ALLEN *brings him his medals*

Medals, Allen, damn ye – deck me out, garnish me – while I tell 'em what they're all for.
ALLEN *helps him on with his medals.*
There's a medal for the Nile, there's a medal for St Vincent, there's the Order of the Bath, there's a Dukedom from the King of Naples, there's a Barony from the King of England –
ALLEN. Baron Nelson of the Nile and of Burnham Thorpe in Norfolk –
NELSON. Cocked hat. Will you get me my cocked hat, man, or I'll kick you from here to Trinidad!

ALLEN *passes him the hat.*

Now pass the word for Captain Hardy. Tell him I want the entire squadron at immediate readiness to proceed to sea. I am about to go to the King: I shan't be long. When I get back I will tell him what it is we have to deal with.
ALLEN. Aye aye sir.

Exit ALLEN. NELSON *preens himself for a moment.*

NELSON. That lascivious little strumpet was in Naples not three days ago. She had been kept there by a young Colonel of the French army of occupation. And he paid her off and sent her packing. Why? Because the army of occupation is in occupation no longer. Being an old acquaintance of mine she came straight to Palermo and told me the news. King

Ferdinand has a chance of returning home at once. I wonder
will he take it ? He's a pot-bellied timorous mountebank:
but by Christ he *is* a King!

He whips out his sword and commences a fantastic dance,
whirling the blade around him in the air. He sings.

> The King of Naples is a King
> And he wears a golden crown
> Who dares to pull it off him
> I will strike the bastard down
> I will strike the bastard down
> I will rip him with my sword
> The King of Naples is a King
> A glorious sovereign lord.

He finishes his dance with a great swoop which takes him across
to the KING, *before whom he falls dramatically on one knee,*
the sword raised in salute.

Your Majesty, as the senior naval commander in these
waters under the authority of His Britannic Majesty King
George, I am honoured to inform you that your capital
city is now at least free of all alien troops.

KING. Why?

NELSON. My informant suggests to me that Bonaparte
regards the so-called Revolutionary Republican Government in Naples as sufficiently well established to look after
its own defences, and he needs his army elsewhere. The
defences of the city are now placed under the charge of
Commodore Caracciolo.

KING and QUEEN. Caracciolo! Traitor! Renegade! Death to
Caracciolo!

NELSON. Exactly so, sir. But he was once your Minister of
Marine: and as such highly competent. Nevertheless he
has not the resources to defend the town against the British
fleet and I propose to attack at once. The Cardinal of
Calabria, as you know, has levied an irregular royalist army

in the mountains and I make no doubt he too will be pressing home the advantage on your Majesty's behalf from the landward side.

KING. Very good very good very good.

QUEEN. So away you go, my brave Lord Nelson.

NELSON. Oh no, your Majesty, pardon me: but you must come too.

KING. What?

NELSON. If I am to take Naples I must be able directly to hand the captured city over to its rightful lord and master. Otherwise – perhaps, Sir William, you will be so good as to explain to the King the diplomatic exigency.

HAMILTON. Ticklish, milord, ticklish – if there is really no French army in Naples then perhaps the original neutrality of the city may still obtain, I don't know. We can't just go blowing it down out of hand: I take it you have received no orders to do so?

NELSON. I have received orders to fall back upon Malta: but I have no intention of obeying them. What, sir, when there is a monarch to be restored to his people – in any case, it is this very ticklish question of neutrality that makes it so imperative that the King should come with us.

HAMILTON. He won't want to come: he is a coward.

KING (*who has been conferring with the* QUEEN – *she apparently urging him to agree with* NELSON, *he resisting her*). No: never never never will I condescend again in Naples to display my resplendent countenance!

QUEEN. But you must, my lord – think of the triumph of your ultimate revenge!

KING. And think of what happened to the head of Queen Marie Antoinette! Marie Antoinette was your sister – in the basket, chop-chop –

NELSON. Sir William, could not your wife do something – ? She has some influence where we have none, and if –

HAMILTON. She's gone to sleep.

NELSON. Then wake her up.

HAMILTON. Er – Mrs Cadogan . . .

MRS CADOGAN. Bored to death and I don't wonder. I always

did maintain that Palermo was nothing if it wasn't provin-
cial. But, come on, lovey, stir yourself, there's Lord Nelson
has a job for you.

She pokes EMMA, *who wakes up sulkily, then sees* NELSON *and
looks charming.*

EMMA. Oh, do pardon me, Lord Nelson, I fear you catch me
at a most ungraceful disadvantage – but what, does my
country's service call me yet again? What is it I must do?
Nelson commands and Emma shall obey.

SIR WILLIAM *whispers in her ear.*

God help us, but of course –

She kisses her husband, flirtatiously looking at NELSON *the
while.*

– and now then – to beard the ogre in his den!

She goes across to the KING.

KING. I will not be brought back to my kingdom under the
amputated armpit of a Lutheran Saxon Admiral! No,
Madam Hamilton, dispose your charms elsewhere!

EMMA (*sings*).
        Most affronted King
        Though you hide your face in dudgeon
        Your ears I will not bludgeon
        It is not to you I sing.

        But your Queen must hear
        Oh Madam, my prayers will move you
        You know how I do love you –
        I am your friend so dear.

QUEEN (*sings*).
> Yes indeed you are:
> But he's like a furious panther
> Confounded in distemper
> Struck dumb with rage and fear.

EMMA (*singing*).
> Then with rage and with fear he must jump on his feet
> And swell in his fury till he be full.
> Strutting the deck of a proud British fleet
> There is not one obstacle left to his will!
>
> What, rage and fear, and grapeshot and powder,
> Set Naples on fire and throw it all down:
> Nelson is with you and Nelson has power
> To kill every soul in that damnable town!

KING (*singing and dancing in a maniac frenzy*).
> Kill them kill them, everyone kill them,
> Strangle them horribly, cut out their bowels,
> I will be with you and I will be doing it,
> Revenge oh revenge – I will make them to howl –
> Howl, let them howl, kill them, kill them, kill them, men,
> women, priests, children, where are the executioners, the
> gaolers, guards, and torturers, the firing-squads, the hang-
> men, the hangmen, the hangmen, the hangmen – ?

He dances round and round like a dervish. Enter HARDY.

NELSON. Ah, Captain Hardy: the very man. We are about to
re-capture Naples; His Majesty, thank heavens, has agreed
to come with us. Now let us concert a plan. The Cardinal's
irregulars ought by now to be making extensive inroads
upon the landward suburbs: when our fleet is in sight the
morale of the rebels will probably fall away entirely so it
will not even be necessary to bombard the harbour. A
swift landing of marines, a rapid attack upon the water-
front batteries, and I make no doubt we shall be in and in
control before the enemy realizes what's hit him.

HARDY. That seems a very reasonable arrangement, my lord.

NELSON. Cool: you are cool, Hardy – why? What is it that you deprecate?

HARDY. Tactically, my lord, nothing – but on the general political question – we have after all no authority to intervene in Naples.

NELSON. I think you may leave me to look after all that.

HARDY. Whatever you think best, my lord.

NELSON. Very good. Captain Nisbet, what are you doing here? You are in command of a hospital ship and a disgraceful un-seamanlike insanitary barge you have reduced her to, I am sorely afraid. So pluck your ideas up, boy, and get yourself ready for action!

NISBET. Yes, father.

NELSON. God's Blood, we are on duty, you call me sir when you speak to me.

NISBET. Aye aye sir.

NELSON. So off you go.

HAMILTON *is dithering about, looking dubious.*

HAMILTON.
> My lord, for whatever you do, you may count on my support:
> Though I do think it best that it should not be thought
> That open countenance to this action has been given
> by the British Government.
> Therefore I will remain in a partial concealment
> Until your usual notorious success becomes apparent.
> If you fail
> And are brought before court-martial, you will the better prevail
> By pleading entire ignorance of the political difficulty.
> I am certain that the celebrated hero of the Nile
> Will be permitted some small measure of foolhardy eccentricity.

Below decks, you see, unwell, not available for consultation . . .

Exeunt HAMILTON *and* NISBET.

EMMA.
> I am not afraid of diplomatic indiscretion:
> I shall remain on the quarter-deck here in full view
> Proud of the danger, proud of the British nation,
> And, most of all, my lord Nelson, I stand here proud
>   of you.

THE FATHER RETURNS TO HIS CHILDREN:

NELSON. Captain Hardy, I'd be obliged if you would weigh anchor directly and make all necessary sail.

HARDY. Aye aye sir. Sailing-master, call hands to the capstan to weigh anchor, if you please.

SAILING-MASTER. Aye aye sir. Bosun, pipe hands to the capstan and no bloody loitering!

BOSUN. Aye aye sir. Come on then, hands to the capstan, get to it, or I'll skin your sterns alive!

The anchor is weighed.

Anchor a-weigh, sir.

SAILING-MASTER. Anchor a-weigh, sir.

HARDY. Thank you, Sailing-master: and now, if you please, we'll have the courses and the topsails set – we can do without the t'gallants until the wind drops a little.

SAILING-MASTER. Aye aye sir. Bosun, all hands to make sail – courses and your topsails!

BOSUN. Set your courses and your topsails, lively now, you idle buggers, heave them halliards smartly, *heave* when you hear the call, *I* see you bloody tailing on at the tail-end like a white-handed parson's clerk, get to it and *heave* . . . *etc., etc.*

SAILORS (*singing*).
> King George's ships are on the tide
> Sing ho for liberty

With our rows of guns on every side
We've come to make you free.

When Nelson comes across the water
Ho for liberty
If you will not refrain from slaughter
He'll not make you free.

Ye cowardly dogs and dagoes
Ho for liberty
Shut your eyes and hold your nose
If we are to make you free.

In Naples city there was a brawl
Ho for liberty
But Nelson he didn't mind that at all
He'd come to make 'em free.

He ordered in his red marines
Sing ho for liberty
And he smashed them all to smithereens
All for to make 'em free.

We caught the chief of all the gang
Sing ho for liberty
And we beat him down with many a bang
We meant to make him free.

We tied his arms with a length of twine
Sing ho for liberty
And we dragged him up at the end of a line
That's how we made him free.

We set him out on the quarter-deck
Sing ho for liberty
And bejasus he looked like a terrible wreck
But he knew that he was free.

During the song the actions described in it have been performed as far as the capacity of the company allows: and now CARAC- CIOLO, *roped and dishevelled, is dragged onto the stage.* NELSON *salutes the* KING, *who has been huddling in shelter throughout the violent action.*

NELSON. I am happy to report to Your Majesty that the city is now entirely under control. Such resistance as the Republicans were able to put up has been rapidly subdued and many prisoners have been taken.

KING. What prisoners? *Chief* Prisoners?

NELSON. Hardy?

HARDY. Persons of considerable rank and station, my lord. Many of them female. The Marines have most of them under guard in warehouses along the water-front. We are awaiting your further orders as to their disposition.

NELSON. Are there any Neapolitan soldiers in the town? I mean loyalist, of course.

HARDY. There's a sort of irregular army, most of them without uniform, they seem to have occupied the principal streets and public buildings.

NELSON. Ah, the Cardinal's men, no doubt.

HARDY. Murderous hooligans, is my opinion, my lord.

NELSON. You are not asked for your opinion, Captain Hardy. Anyway, your prisoners are to be handed over to some responsible officer of the Cardinal's force.

HARDY. But sir –

NELSON. Will you see to it, please, at once.

HARDY. And Caracciolo?

NELSON. Aha, so we have him! For His Majesty, that one.

KING (*sings*).

> Here is the dog that bites the ballocks off his father
> Here is the swordfish that splits his mother's womb:
> Give him to me: I'll put my thumbnails in his eyeballs:
> Give him to me and I will dance upon his tomb!

He throws himself at CARACCIOLO *but* HARDY *prevents him.*

HARDY. One moment, sir, if you please.

NELSON. Hardy!

HARDY. Your pardon, my lord, but Commodore Caracciolo claims that he surrendered himself upon regular conditions. I must respectfully submit that nothing can be done to him except in a correct and formal fashion.

KING. What! But Lord Nelson, I was *promised* the death of this man!

NELSON. He surrendered upon conditions? To whom did he surrender?

HARDY. To the Cardinal of Calabria, my lord.

Enter the CARDINAL.

CARDINAL. Do not speak, your Majesty, until you have heard me out, I beg. My negotiations with Commodore Caracciolo have saved for your Majesty very many loyal lives. I would therefore desire your Majesty to ratify the terms I offered and to extend an appropriate clemency at least to the wives and families of the leading Republicans who are in danger at this moment from the patriotic enthusiasm of my violent and barbarous troops.

KING *gobbles with rage.*

NELSON. By whose authority, sir, did you offer these terms?

CARDINAL. I could call upon no authority but my own. Was not the King in Palermo?

NELSON. Then your own authority is no authority: and that's enough of *you.* Your Majesty: Caracciolo: does your Majesty want him hanged?

KING. Strangled . . . very slowly!

HARDY. But my lord, we can't just have him lynched.

NELSON. Lynched? What is lynched?

HARDY. It is an Irish word, my lord. It means – ah – well – more or less – it means murdered.

EMMA. And are not the Irish themselves the greatest murderers and rebels on God's earth?

MRS CADOGAN. Oh but dearie, wait a minute – Commodore
Caracciolo is a most cultivated gentleman – why in the old
days he often had his dinner with Sir William and you and
me, and you'd talk about poetry and your Roman architec-
ture and all the classical elegancies – and in those days, of
course, Naples was nothing if not elegant . . .

CARACCIOLO. Naples, gracious lady, was dear to the heart of
everyone. But you do wrong to hold *me* responsible for the
condition it is in now. My efforts, perhaps mistaken, and
certainly ill-fated, were directed to no other end but to
prevent such a circumstance.

> Naples is my city and I did
> Believe it was the loveliest on earth:
> As it were a goddess stretched out on a bed
> Between the sea from which she had her birth,
> Between the pure blue sea and the green mountains
> Her limbs lay lazy on a coverlet:
> Upon her neck, her breast, her golden loins,
> A hundred rare and glaring jewels were set
> To catch the sun and throw it back again
> As bright or brighter than her own black eyes:
> For years I sat and worshipped her in a dream,
> My idle hand caressed her idle thighs –
> I was in love, I asked no question –
> Until one day the wind blew a cross flaw,
> The coverlet was disturbed with that quick motion
> Just up, and down; my eyes moved, and I saw
> The bed on which she lay. Not rocks, nor flowers,
> Not coral pink and white: but rotten bones
> And half-chewed limbs and dripping eyes and ears,
> Skulls, bladders, children's feet, and I heard groans
> And bubbling cries, and there were rats and snakes
> Among the corpses – not every corpse was dead –
> And this was a great foul heap, where I would make
> My thoughtless languorous love to her. She had lice
> in her head.

HARDY. Who did?

CARACCIOLO. She was a goddess. She had lice in her head.

I did not discover it until that moment. They were creeping up out of the pile of filth and climbing into her hair. (*He points suddenly to the* KING *and the* QUEEN.) There's one of them: and there's another! And the wind that did reveal them blew straight to Naples out of France. How long before the French wind turns about and reaches England, Admiral Nelson? Will you English see what I saw when your own bedspreads are lifted up? You said right, madam – like the Irish. Oh, the Irishmen have quick eyes, and sensitive nostrils too.

EMMA (*throwing herself on him, dragging him down, and singing*).

> Do not you speak of Irish men –
> I am myself of Irish blood:
> I know the murderous heart that beats
> At large within the poisoned wood.
> I know those men of Irish land,
> With Frenchmen's power they did up-rear –
> They killed the baby in the womb,
> And plundered house and home and tower!
>
> When men are turned to wild beasts
> To wild beasts they turn us all:
> Tear off his clothes and beat him down
> On four bare feet on the ground let him crawl!
> Let him crawl and wallow like a swine,
> Grub up the grass and root the dung:
> Then cut his throat and singe his bristles,
> On the butcher's hook let him be hung!

HARDY. My lord, we are in uniform – Caracciolo is in his own uniform – we cannot permit –

CARDINAL. Sir – consider the broken and pitiful condition of this once honourable and always courageous officer –

NELSON (*sings*).

> Oh I know he's a poor old tottering creature
> With a crumpled face and thin gray hair:
> His withered heart still beats with passion –
> Who am I to say it is not sincere?

But let him live and a hundred like him
As fierce as he, but not so old,
Will fill their own fresh hearts with courage
And serve up their lives into Bonaparte's hold.

He's the rotten patch in the fair green apple,
The drip of water through the leaking keel,
The stink of gangrene in a clean-cut sword-wound
To warn us all that it will not heal –

Oh, *I* know about that well enough – you don't imagine for one moment that they took off my arm in a brief and painless fashion? Lady Hamilton has convinced me with her recollection of Ireland: we had our own abundant treason there, in ninety-eight, and it was, thank heaven, nipped in the bud! But, Captain Hardy has a scruple which I think is a just one. Caracciolo is an officer – he cannot hang without trial. A court-martial composed of other officers of the Neapolitan service – Your Majesty will no doubt find it easy to choose them? And at once, if you please, sir: we must have him dead before sunset. So take him away.

CARACCIOLO *is led away.* HARDY *goes with him.*

CARDINAL. This is not only vindictive – it is also very unwise. Your Majesty must understand that you cannot reimpose your popularity by brute force.

KING. If you do not hold your tongue I shall have you hanged as well – liberal!

QUEEN. My lord, I beg you, on my knees, for God's sake do not abuse the Cardinal of Calabria – he is the only Magnifico of Naples who is still upon our side!

KING. I know that very well, madam: and for you the rest of my loyal Magnificoes and their wives, and their children if they have any – they are all of them to be strangled: Lord Nelson has very kindly given orders to his marines to hand the prisoners over to me. Lord Nelson, you have my gratitude: and now there is to be feasting, and music, and fireworks: we mean to celebrate our great revenge. Madam, do you come?

EMMA. Dear Madam, do not weep. For who needs any longer the Magnificoes of Naples? You have Nelson: it is enough.

The KING *and* QUEEN *go out;* NELSON, *with* EMMA *on his arm, is about to follow them, when he stops with a sudden hesitation. The* CARDINAL *goes out with the* KING.

NELSON. It is my head. It is a pain as though someone was driving an icicle into it – here.

EMMA. It's that wound again, oh God but I thought it was quite better. Take your hat off. Why do you have to wear it all the time? It is so heavy.

NELSON. This plume was presented me by the Sultan of Turkey as a reward for the victory of the Nile. It works by clockwork.

EMMA. Nelson, my dear man, I know all about the plume . . . Look here, what *is* the matter? We must go to the King's banquet.

NELSON. I am sorry: it is a little easier now – but dear Emma, you *will* sit next to me, and cut my meat up and so forth, and keep an eye open in case I feel faint – or –

EMMA. – or get drunk?

NELSON. No no, not get drunk, my servant Allen takes care of all that – if I put my hand upon one glass too many, he will clear his throat – like this: ha h'm – and then, don't you see, I will know not to take any more . . .

HE DOES NOT KNOW AND SHE DOES NOT KNOW:

Enter ALLEN.

ALLEN. Ha h'm . . .

Dance music heard as though from a distance. NELSON *and* EMMA *begin to dance.*

The King of Naples' banquet being held in the great cabin, up here on the quarter-deck is a fair enough place to dance, with the sun going down all clear and rapid into the purple water of the Mediterranean, and just enough wind

blowing to keep away the mosquitoes. Do you think, as
I think, that that pain in his head is more in the nature of an
alibi? Listen to that then – !

*Screams of terror and brutal laughter – some people are hunted
out by the* KING's *supporters and chased mockingly about till
they are caught: then they are put to death with callous abandon.*

Quite a lot going on for which we need an alibi just at the
present – what do you say, Captain Nisbet, sir?

NISBET *is passing across the stage.*

NISBET.
> The King of Naples is a King
> He wears a golden crown:
> He bears the burden all alone
> For all that happens in his town.
> A naval officer is not permitted
> In foreign politics to be committed:
> What he does may be distasteful or it may be jolly
>   good fun,
> But he needs no sort of an alibi if his duty is properly
>   done.

Exit NISBET. *A gun is fired.* NELSON *and* EMMA *stop dancing
for a moment and stand apart: then suddenly they come together
again and continue as before though their movements are now
less formal and more sensual.*

ALLEN. Ah there he goes Caracciolo dead! Haul him up to
the good old yardarm – a British yardarm moreover ...
Not but what he *did* have these pains often enough before
and they were genuine without a doubt. And she *did* nurse
him very tenderly in that Embassy bedroom ...

(*He sings.*)

> His wound is not so sorely inflamed
> That on its rage must his deeds be blamed:
> The blood that throbbed hot against his skull
> Is throbbing now inside the nurse's tail.

Did he infect her with it the first,
Put fire in her flesh till it all but burst?
Her eyes are red where they should be white
And the cloth of his breeches has suddenly grown tight.

Yet he does not know and she does not know
Why the politics of Naples disturb them so:
Yet sure if they did, they would think it wrong
That to get them to bed a man must hang.

Another gun fires.

Sunset. Now then it'll be time they unhitch him from the noose and put weights upon his feet and drop him into the water.

NELSON *and* EMMA *have stopped dancing and go out.*

Yerss, they'll be off to see it done. Felt kind of squeamish about bearing witness to the execution itself: but that don't signify: he'll be getting a full report of it in all its details from old Hardy or some other long-nosed meddler.

YOU CAN'T ARGUE WITH A DEAD MAN:

Develop underwater spectacle.

ALLEN. I'd better get along out of it if I don't want to be drowned. Oh-oh, there he is – wouldn't you just expect it of a bunch of useless eyeties – they haven't put the right weights on him and the silly bastard won't sink.

CARACCIOLO'*s body comes drifting down from above, feet first, his head cocked over on one side.* ALLEN *climbs a ladder and goes out, above. Lights from the fireworks distort the underwater light.*

VOICE OF DEAD CARACCIOLO. Protect the poor people of Naples. Give heart to the poor people. Let them have the courage to understand their poverty. Drive out their enemies: defend them from their friends.

NELSON *enters above and climbs painfully down the ladder to the stage.*

NELSON. I was their friend. I still am their friend. I brought them back their King.

VOICE OF DEAD CARACCIOLO. I brought them their liberty.

NELSON. You brought them in the Frenchmen. *I* brought them their liberty.

VOICE OF DEAD CARACCIOLO. Your liberty carries the great cannon – seventy-five, eighty, one hundred to every ship.

NELSON. And yours fills up a black basket with a pile of bleeding heads.

VOICE OF DEAD CARACCIOLO. So which of us is right?

NELSON. I refuse, absolutely, to argue with a dead man
>   When you were alive, you had every opportunity
>   To put these equivocal questions to my own face, directly:
>   Instead of which all you gave us was your preoccupation
>   With naked women – upon beds and so forth – which in your position
>   And at your advanced age I can only regard
>   As a pitiful delirium and far better ignored.

You make me ashamed for you, sir: disgusted I was – yes.

VOICE OF DEAD CARACCIOLO. At me – or at yourself?

NELSON *(becoming incoherent)*. Certainly not – not – most emphatically not at myself – !
>   But people will believe you, won't they,
>   Simply because you are dead!
>   Don't you all see that he is lying:
>   Will you look at the sanctimonious crook of his false head!
>   I am not lying and I am still alive:
>   Is there nobody here, nobody, who will listen to me and believe?

EMMA *climbs in down the ladder.*

EMMA. Oh what has poor Horace done that he should be sent away to sea when his health was so bad and his stature so small?

For the whole of his life he must travel the salt water
Where his only true love was King Neptune's fish-
tailed-daughter –

(*She sings.*)

To the Eastern Ocean he must go
Though the fever shook his bones
In his hammock wrapped up like a stillborn child
They sadly brought him home.

He would not rest, he would not stay,
Once more he must set forth:
'I nearly died in the East,' he cried,
'So I'll go to the Arctic North.'

But half the height of the gun he held
There was nothing he would not dare
He walked out alone across the ice
And he fought the great white bear.

NELSON (*sings*).
He fought the French and the Spaniards too
For years and years he fought:
He lost his arm and he lost his eye –

EMMA (*sings*).
But he never lost his heart.

NELSON.
That is not true: as very well you know.
On an island of the Caribbees I met with a fair young
widow:
I married her: and when they cut off my arm
She stood at my bed's head and she guarded me from
harm.
I lived with her so many years:
I shall live with her again.
She stood at my bed's head
And soothed away my pain . . .
I can't abide to be in pain. . . . Do you suppose *he* was in
pain when they hanged him?

EMMA.

> He went to his death with complete insensitivity
> He had entirely abandoned all civilized morality
> Not one friend gave a cheer for him as he dangled
>   above the tide
> He might have been a sack of flour or a bundle of
>   waterlogged wood.

NELSON.

> Stubborn and dull
> Oh a brutal old fool
> And a two-leggèd mule
> Yet bold he was, bold,
> High-hearted and cold –
> Why would he not speak?
> They said that he did walk
> Counting his feet
> Bolt upright to meet
> The clutch of the rope:
> I have no hope
> That I could face
> Such grave disgrace
> So brave as that.
> I would fall flat
> On the plank of the deck
> Spew up thick sick
> Down my foul shirt
> Roll in my own dirt
> Groan moan and gibber
> For helpless terror –
> That is how it would be
> Were they to bring me
> And my name, my acclaim,
> My accredited fame,
> To an ending of such shame.
> Caracciolo knew
> What he had to do:
> And he did it in my despite.
> He was so certain he was right.

I knew it too:
And so did you –
Why else were we so cruel?

VOICE OF DEAD CARACCIOLO.

Because you are both English and you could not endure
To see a brave man of Naples murdered by English
    power.

EMMA.

If you weep in your uniform all your medals of honour
Will be stained and corroded by the fall of salt water:
Oh my dear oh my darling, this is no disaster –
For the cowardly King is saved from the courage of
    his own traitor.

NELSON. Emma: I am not a hangman – I *am* a bold brave
sailor!

(*He sings.*)

I fought the French and the Spaniards too
For years and years I fought:
I knew no fear for I persevered
In the duty that I was taught.

I heard no questions but just one:
Had I done all that could be done?
Until this day, oh the answer came clear:
'Not yet not yet, but persevere'.

And now, for the first time, I have found there is another
question: persevere, persevere, persevere *where* . . . ?

VOICE OF DEAD CARACCIOLO. Where?

NELSON *falls into a frenzy and swears and curses all over the
shop.* CARACCIOLO's *body is drawn up, and off. Underwater
lighting dissolves.*

EMMA. He has floated up – he doesn't answer – oh look at
you, look at you, cursing and swearing and with no notion
of what to do . . .

NO, BUT A WILD NEW VOYAGE:

She takes him in her arms.

EMMA. You are at the end of your voyage in Naples: on where will you wander now ... ? Who is to set you your new course, who is to find you the charts on which to mark it ... ?

LORD KEITH *enters. He carries a letter.* NELSON *and* EMMA *separate quickly.*

KEITH. You will not need any charts, my lord. Your new voyage is overland. I have here the orders for your recall to England: purely upon grounds of ill health, you understand.

NELSON. Do I? Do I, my lord? You are Commander-in-Chief of the Mediterranean Fleet and I am no more than a subordinate Rear-Admiral, so – I am aware that it must appear that I have not precisely obeyed all your orders to the letter: but I am quite certain I can justify my proceedings before any court-martial that you determine to convoke.

KEITH. My lord, no-one is talking or even thinking of a court-martial. The wound in your head is well-known to be a lingering one: therefore, prolonged leave, at home in England, until you are completely cured. I trust you will give my affectionate regards to dear Lady Nelson, when you meet her.

He gives the orders to NELSON, *and exit. Enter* HAMILTON, *also carrying a letter.*

HAMILTON. I am said to be in bad health. I am also said to be old. They have therefore recalled me to London. In disgrace? No, not exactly. Old age and poor health, that is all ... Do we travel overland, or by sea?

NELSON. I am not permitted a warship in which to fly my flag back to England. It says so: it says so here.

HAMILTON. So overland then. It will not be comfortable.

NELSON. No.

HAMILTON *retires and sits quietly at the back of the stage.*

EMMA. My God it is a deliberate insult!

NELSON. There are very few ships to spare. I think it can be justified, upon tactical considerations . . .

EMMA. Nelson: we were not talking about tactical considerations.

NELSON (*sings*).

No: but a wild new voyage
Quite unmarked on any chart:
To hell with my seasick stomach –
I embark with undaunted heart.

In London they will praise me
For all the Frenchmen whom I killed
In London they will praise me
For the orders I would not fulfil.

In London they will praise me
As I have been by the Grand Turk
See, I will wind his mechanical plume:
Let them gape as they watch it work!

He winds up the mechanical plume and struts about the stage while it whirs upon his hat.

Let them gape as I stand by the woman
Whom I love in the glare of the sun:
Not one woman: two: I'm a hero
They love me: I love them: it is done!

EMMA (*sings*).

It is done, and declared: you have said it.

NELSON (*sings*).

I gave up one arm and one eye:
A second gay lady to love me
It is all I have left till I die!
The Grand Turk would surely permit it –

EMMA.

Good God you wear his hat –
Oh you greedy fierce tom-cat –

NELSON.

> I have whiskers teeth and claws
> And I live by my own laws . . .

This time he takes the amorous initiative and kisses her with great abandon.

EMMA. And he grappled and boarded her, swarming the huge side of her majestical bulk as ardent and as valorous as when at the Battle of St Vincent he had led his marines in triumph across the decks of one great Spanish ship and from thence upon another one, until both of them had struck their colours and lay rolling on the long dull waves, entirely given over to his uttermost desire . . .

> And shall you then love me as much as you love her?

NELSON.

> Shall you then love her as much as I love you?

EMMA.

> And shall you love Sir William as much as you love me?

HAMILTON *comes forward.*

HAMILTON. I am sad to leave Naples, even though it be in the company of one whom, I protest, I love as much as any man it has ever been my good fortune to meet.

> Now that we have between us
> Brought the fire of mortal war
> Upon the slopes of cold Vesuvius
> There is nothing more for me to do
> Except I give my arm to you,
> And you will take it – there we are –
> And, Emma, you take mine:
> And so, we stand in line,
> And follow, like the Three Wise Men,
> Our strange and unpredicted star.

They march out. As they do so, the KING *speaks from above.*

KING.

> We are glad to see them gone.

Naples now can stand alone.
The power of England on the sea
With our great Catholic power does not agree.
Caracciolo never need have died
Had Nelson not been yelping at my side.
Therefore, the blame, if any blame remain,
Must fall on Nelson's headstrong head: not mine.
My people all: rejoice with cheerful shout:
Your King is in: the Englishmen are out!

Neapolitan cheers.

Act Two

Enter NISBET.

NISBET. Upon Lord Nelson's arrival in London they filled
every street with carnival! And what came they out into
the wilderness to see? The man who hanged Caracciolo?
God help us, out of one hundred in that multitude there
might possibly be a single informed person who had at least
a notion of who Caracciolo was.

(*He sings.*)

> For had they all known who he was –
> Being ragged dirty British skin-and-bone –
> It is just possible they would have cried
> For a bold Caracciolo of their own.
>
> It is just possible but not much more:
> We live upon an island, as you know,
> We're proud of that, however poor we are,
> We're proud of it and want to keep it so.
>
> A little island in our island home
> Is made of stone: they call it Newgate Gaol.
> We have a floating island made of wood:
> The fleet that won the Battle of the Nile.
>
> If you don't like the one, then try the other:
> The King and Parliament have made quite sure
> That angry ragged men have no third choice –
> We're on an island and we are at war.
>
> The noble Governor of Newgate Gaol

Is not acclaimed by thousands in the street:
But when the Victor of the Nile comes home
Red roses bloom beneath his sacred feet.

NELSON, HAMILTON, EMMA *and* MRS CADOGAN *walk among cheering crowds who strew red rose-petals before them. Their positions are now changed, so that* EMMA *now walks in the middle with a man on each arm.*

THE PEOPLE (*singing*).

Join we great Nelson's name
First on the roll of fame;
Him let us sing!
Spread we his praise around
Honour of British ground
Who made Nile's shores resound:
God save our King.

NELSON. The people, of all sorts and conditions, have rendered us a great welcome, which has moved me to tears. Yet at the Admiralty there was no such enthusiasm, and from His Majesty King George, I regret, not one word. . . . It is an extraordinary thing that my wife is not here to greet us. Josiah: why have we not heard from your dear mother?

NISBET. And why has my dear mother not heard from *you*?

NELSON. Where's Allen? Allen!

Enter ALLEN

ALLEN. Milord?

NELSON. Have you any conception what Lady Nelson intends?

ALLEN. No doubt she will intend what you intended her to intend, milord.

NELSON. What, what, what – what the devil do you mean, sir? Explain yourself directly – Where is she? Josiah – do *you* know?

NISBET. No.

ALLEN. Milord – ?

NELSON. Oh do be quiet, you silly man! It is intolerably humiliating not to be received by one's own wife upon so momentous a homecoming. I told her to be present at –

ALLEN. You told her to be present at the hotel in Piccadilly, milord, notwithstanding her own expressed wish that you should call in to her at home in Norfolk upon your route to town from Yarmouth.

NISBET. So that's where she will be.

NELSON. The hotel – ?

ALLEN. In Piccadilly.

NELSON. Then why the deuce could you not say so? Is this the way to Piccadilly?

ALLEN. No milord, *this* way.

NELSON. I am perfectly capable of setting a course across London. I refuse to be treated like some sort of baby . . .

Exit NELSON, *the rest following dispersedly.*
The CROWD *breaks up and clears away.*

THE HEROINE SINGS OF A BRIGHT-WINGED BIRD:

Enter LADY NELSON.

LADY NELSON. Surely Lord Nelson should have arrived in town by now. Of course the Yarmouth stage-coach would be met by enormous crowds and it would be difficult for him to break away from them all at once. I do hope that the public enthusiasm will not lead him to behave in an unsuitable fashion – oh, why could he not have travelled directly to Norfolk? When he is not at sea, a quiet rural existence is the only sort of life to which he is fitted: and he knows that very well, if he would only stop to think. Please God let him not forget those happy days we had before the war –

(*She sings.*)

> Through green fields and meadows we ofttimes did walk
> And sweet conversation of love we did talk
> While the birds in the woodland so sweetly did sing
> And the lovely thrush voices made the valleys to ring.

But his letters from the Mediterranean have of late been
cold and formal, and my Josiah has also written me some
very strange letters – who *is* this Lady Hamilton, and what
can she have to do with so modest a gentleman as is my dear
husband; Yet I must not be apprehensive: Horatio was
ever the body and soul of loyalty. . . .

(*She sings.*)

> Although my love seem distant I will not be cast down
> I know that my sailor has once more returned
> He will make me amends for my trouble and strife
> And I and my true love will be happy for life.

Enter NELSON.

Horatio – !

NELSON. Fanny.

LADY NELSON. My dear husband: my beloved, unpunctual
husband: at last you are in my arms!

NELSON. Fanny: why were you not at the stage-coach to meet
me? You have made me look particularly foolish in front
of my good friends the Hamiltons.

LADY NELSON. Oh my dearest love. They will not mind, I
am sure, not if Lady Hamilton is as delightful a person as
you have told me in your letters.

NELSON. Oh indeed, my love, she is. She is longing to meet
you. I have told her that –

LADY NELSON. When do we go to Norfolk? Tonight?

NELSON. Tonight? Oh – scarcely possible – my dear Fanny.

LADY NELSON. I have had so many improvements carried
out upon the new house, I know how you must be anxious
to hear of them all. First of all, the kitchen pump –

NELSON. Now, Fanny, just one moment –

The HAMILTONS *and* MRS CADOGAN *enter, with* NISBET
slouching along behind them.

EMMA. Nelson! Where is Nelson? Nelson, we can wait no
longer – do you forget we are promised forth?

LADY NELSON. Forth.

NELSON. There is a society invitation of some sort – I do
not know what – Fanny: Lady Hamilton, Sir William Hamilton. My dear friends, here is my wife!

MRS CADOGAN (*bursting forth and embracing* LADY NELSON).
Oh the sweet creature, no: I am so delighted!

NELSON. Ah: Mrs Cadogan: Lady Hamilton's mother.

LADY NELSON. But Horatio, the kitchen pump.

EMMA. The what?

LADY NELSON. I was endeavouring to tell you all about the
kitchen pump.

EMMA (*sings*).

    Oh God she is just as I thought she would be
    With the pump and the kitchen and her cups of weak
        tea,
    Yet clearly she loves him: he has loved her in return
    With her hook in his neck and her chain round his groin.
Yet I promised him I would make the effort and God damn
my greedy wicked womb, I will –

(*She sings.*)

    Now poor bashful Nelson, I kiss your sweet wife
    He has told me so much of you, you are part of my life –
    Put your arms in my arms and your cheek against mine
    For I bring home your conqueror to old London town.

LADY NELSON. Lady Hamilton, I am indeed so very pleased
to make your acquaintance. I do hope you will forgive me
my momentary distraction but to be sure I had received no
forewarning of your arrival. Now this invitation: it is to be a
party? We must go to it, of course, though Horatio is very
tired and I myself am far from well. . . .

She catches sight of NISBET.

Josiah – ! My darling boy! How splendid he looks in his
fine Captain's uniform! And how has he behaved?

NELSON. Ah – yes – behaved. . . . He has most certainly
improved. . . . I have a small errand I would like you to
run, my boy, if you could give me your attention for more
than half a minute. It is most important that the newspapers

should be properly informed of my movements when in town.

NISBET (*sings*).

> I could tell of a few movements
> They would never have dreamed:
> How they rocked, in his cabin-hammock
> How she kicked her heels and screamed!

NELSON. Go along, sir, do not loiter – to the newspaper offices, if you please!

Exit NISBET.

Now then, are we all together? We have this party to attend, our good host must not be kept waiting – Emma, upon my left arm; Fanny, upon my – ah, yes, ha h'm . . .

EMMA (*sings as they walk around*).

> When Nelson sang the praises
> Of the wife he'd left behind
> I oft would ask him what it was
> That brought her most to mind:
>
> The foaming crest of the tide in flood,
> The red sun through the rain,
> Or did he see the white lily blow
> On the banks of the Appenine?
>
> 'Oh neither the tide nor the sun,' he cried,
> 'Nor the lily in its bloom –
> But I see her like the bright-winged bird
> That swoops over my jib-boom.'
>
> A land bird or a sea bird she,
> Between the wave and the wind –
> The man of blood on the quarter-deck
> With her music filled his mind!

ATTITUDES OF A HEROINE:

They all march around, now joined by ALLEN, *who brings up the rear until they are greeted by their* HOST.

HOST. My dear Lord Nelson, oh, divine, divine – I had not ventured to believe that you would grace our little entertainment in person. . . . Sir William, I am eternally devoted – Lady Hamilton – Gad, 'tis the Cyprian Goddess with the mutilated Hercules at her tail –

NELSON. Excuse me, I am desirous to present Lady Nelson to you, sir. Fanny, my dear, this is – damn it all, I don't know who it is. . . . Allen, take our hats and so forth.

ALLEN. Will you look at that champagne? I wonder if I dare start the throat-clearing routine tonight? He's stamped down on it pretty crushing every time I've tried it lately . . .

The PRINCE *and other* GUESTS *approach. The* HOST *makes introductions.*

HOST. We have royalty with us tonight, my lord – His Royal Highness the Prince of –

PRINCE. Damme sir, you are impeding a clear view of England's Darling! Ha, Nelson, we are on fire, sir, to shake you by the hand! Lady Nelson, quite delighted, how proud you must be, ma'am – Sir William Hamilton, pleased to meet ye – Lady Hamil— oh yes, quite so –

He dexterously avoids having to meet EMMA, *walks round rapidly and speaks to another* GUEST.

Can't have that, y'know, they wouldn't look at her at Windsor – great mistake, really, bringing the woman here . . .

NELSON (*upset but determined to enjoy himself*). I think we had better get on to the champagne – what are we waiting for? Where's the champagne – Fanny, my dear, you will take a glass? Here you are –

LADY NELSON. No Horatio, I think not: it scarcely agrees with me, and I have not been at all well lately – did I not tell you in my letters?

NELSON. Yes, my dear, you did: but on this occasion, surely –

LADY NELSON. No, Horatio, please. . . . And you yourself have been positively forbidden it by very many doctors – Allen, do tell his lordship that he really ought not –

ALLEN *clears his throat.*

NELSON. Allen, damn your eyes, this is neither the time nor the place –

EMMA. Sir William, my dear, do you know any of these people?

HAMILTON. Oh no. Do not you?

EMMA. I do not, and I don't wish to. But at least they have plenty to drink. Nelson: Nelson, do you hear me! Why are you not taking your champagne? You must have your champagne. Fanny, my sweetheart, he must have his champagne!

MRS CADOGAN (*to* LADY NELSON). It's ever since he had his wound, your ladyship, he's been perfectly dependent on my Emma for knowing what he ought to take and I must say some of her remedies are that quaint, you can't think: but always she knows best.

LADY NELSON. Oh dear, I am sure I am so out of touch: I do not know what to do for the best.

EMMA (*taking* NELSON *aside*). You know what sort of a bird she really is, don't you, Nelson?

NELSON. What? Excuse me for one moment, Your Royal Highness, I – what is it, Emma?

EMMA. A tom-tit. It's just come to me. I beg your pardon, Your Royal Highness, I didn't really intrude, because after all I'm not here . . .

NELSON. Are you talking about Fanny? A tom-tit? That is most unkind of you –

EMMA. But does it suit her or doesn't it? Just look at her – see: this is the way she goes . . .

She commences an imitation of LADY NELSON's *gait and her characteristic bob of the head as she talks.* NELSON *is at first shocked but cannot stop himself from laughing.*

HOST. Why, Lady Hamilton, are you dancing? Will you not be persuaded to give us all the great pleasure of a regular exhibition? The Attitudes, my dear, we are all longing to see them – Sir William, your dear wife, will perform her famous Attitudes, surely she won't refuse?

EMMA. But I don't want to do any Attitudes – Good God, I'm not a cabaret girl!

NELSON. But I adore your Attitudes –

EMMA. Then I shall do them for *you* – and if anyone else cares to peep over your shoulder, they'll be very welcome, I'm sure.

She retires.

PRINCE. Good God, but she's a whopper, though – I'm looking forward to these Attitudes – dancing naked on the tables!

A GUEST. Only purpose the woman has, to undo a few hooks and eyes –

ANOTHER GUEST. I wonder if she's been doing it since she got married?

PRINCE. I bloody well hope so –

ALLEN. Oh she'd do it now all right, if they pumped enough French fizz into her – but God help us, that was years ago – I'm afraid if we get anything tonight it'll be all classical and statuesque . . .

HAMILTON (*claps his hands to attract attention*). Lady Hamilton's Attitudes are, as you know, both classical and statuesque.

ALLEN. Didn't I just tell you?

HAMILTON. She will require to prepare herself for a few moments: in the meantime, pray let me explain how each Attitude is derived from one or other piece of antique decoration from my collection of ceramics. The particular poses that Lady Hamilton will perform tonight illustrate the Fortunes of War. She will impersonate –

PRINCE. Stop drivelling, man, and let her do it!

NELSON. Where are your manners, sir? Be silent, if you please!

PRINCE. Oh: beg your pardon, I'm sure . . .

HAMILTON *and* MRS CADOGAN *prepare a little stagecloth for the Attitudes, and set out a property basket containing a sword, a torch, a crown and a helmet – all in the Grecian style.*

HAMILTON. Lady Hamilton will impersonate, first, the Spirit of Peace aware of the Threat of Strife.

MRS CADOGAN. Oh I am that dumbfoundered how my pretty little Emma has come along so amazing since the days of her perilous infancy. Who that could have looked at her then would conceive of her present gentility? Even the very servants now speak of her as they would of a Duchess . . .

EMMA *enters, with a large veil or stole draped around the shoulders of her gown. She takes her stand on the stagecloth, where* HAMILTON *hands her the props for her Attitudes.* ALLEN *and* MRS CADOGAN *take up positions downstage at the extreme corners.*

ALLEN (*sings*).
>   She was barely more than twelve year old
>   When first upon her back she was rolled.

MRS CADOGAN (*sings*).
>   For the loss of her sweet virginity
>   I wept such great round tears of pity.

Attitude 1: *Properties – stole only.*

HAMILTON. The Spirit of Peace aware of the threat of Strife.

EMMA (*sings*).
>   But hist, hark, where all has been serene
>   I hear the rumbling thunder and the lightning flash
>   doth gleam.

MRS CADOGAN (*sings*).
>   She sadly left her cottage home
>   It is said with a gentleman's babe in her womb.

ALLEN (*sings*).
>   Them gentlemen how they stripped her down
>   How they tossed and humped her around and round.

Attitude 2: *Properties – sword, torch and stole.*

HAMILTON. Strife Triumphant.

EMMA (*sings*).
>   The blade I bear splits mother from her child
>   The brand I wave with acrid spark so wild

Shall fire the roof of cabin, house, and hall:
And where I walk, there tens of thousands fall.
MRS CADOGAN (*sings*).
          Her naked limbs being on display
          On my old knees I knelt to pray.
ALLEN (*sings*).
          Upon her own knees she did tumble:
          Her pretty little bum was pink and humble.

Attitude 3: Properties – sword, helmet and stole.
HAMILTON. The Resurgence of Peace in the guise of National
   Valour.
EMMA (*sings*).
          No no, no no, the time for sloth is gone:
          Revenge doth rage, th'aroused blood must burn.
MRS CADOGAN (*sings*).
          Then a gentleman paid good money down
          For to have her love him all the time.
ALLEN (*sings*).
          Such an answer to a mother's prayer:
          He tickled her fast and he tickled her fair.

Attitude 4: Properties – helmet and stole.

HAMILTON. Peace weeps for the Victims of Strife.
EMMA (*sings*).
          Alas they are all dead, how shall we know
          How many innocents have gone below?
          But with them go the guilty in their crime:
          Rejoice and mourn both at the self-same time.
MRS CADOGAN (*sings*).
          But his passion waned and she was sent
          To his uncle's house on the Continent,
          Which was the British Embassy –
          And soon an Ambassador's wife was she.

Attitude 5: Properties – helmet, stole and crown.

HAMILTON. And finally, Victory crowns the Victorious Hero.
   The crown, you will observe, is ornamented with the beaks

or rostra of the captured enemy warships, after the pattern
of the ancient imperial and republican trophies ...

EMMA. I can't do this without a hero – where is he ? Sit him
down – Nelson!

GUESTS. Nelson!

NELSON *comes forward sheepishly and plants himself down at
her feet. Great cheers.*
NISBET *(drunk) enters at about this time.*

NELSON. Mrs Siddons – and I make this statement solemnly –
Mrs Siddons be damned!

EMMA *(sings).*
>   We crown the Ruler of the Sea:
>   Old Neptune bows on bended knee,
>   Leaping dolphins in their pride
>   Conturb the wreckage of the tide:
>   Each wave precurrent now must roar –
>   All hail all hail, the Victor of the War!

She puts the crown on NELSON'*s head. More cheers.*

ALLEN *(sings).*
>   So old and pale her husband grew
>   She could not teach him all she knew,
>   He would not rise for rub nor scrub
>   He lay like flannel in the old wash-tub –
>   Her body clothed, her body bare,
>   There was nowt he could do but gape and stare,
>   So in the end he must contrive
>   To shew her to the world and stand aside.

*The last two lines of his song are picked up as a jigging chorus
by all the Guests and the party threatens to become a riot.*
HAMILTON *picks up the prop basket and stage cloth and makes a
discreet exit.*
LADY NELSON *suddenly thrusts herself forward towards her
husband.*

LADY NELSON. Horatio – the charades are now over – will
you please take off that silly crown!

NELSON. Fanny – was that you – ? What the devil do you mean ?

EMMA. I know what she means.

NELSON. Both Lady Hamilton and her husband are my very dear friends and you must learn to love them both: as I do. Emma, you do love me ? You do love my wife ?

EMMA. I have endeavoured to do so. She has not helped to make it easy.

NELSON. Carry on – perform some more Attitudes, sing something – dance – ?

HAMILTON. Yes, dance, my dear, dance –

PRINCE. Choreography, terpsichore, get her legs in the air, let her dance –

GUESTS. Get her legs in the air!

EMMA. The Tarantella? Oh the greatest thing about the Tarantella is that it is an expression of scorn –

NISBET. Mother, you must tell him. It is not right and you must tell him. Do you not know that he has said he wants to *marry* her ?

LADY NELSON. I cannot believe it: will not believe it: he is a man of so much honour.

EMMA *dances the Tarantella, with tambourine.*

NELSON *joins in the dance too, in a wild and untrained fashion. Now they take* LADY NELSON *and compel her to dance too. She does her best but faintness overcomes her and she falls weakly onto* NISBET's *arm to be led away.* NELSON *has not noticed and he and* EMMA *go on spinning wildly until exhausted. The* GUESTS *are standing round them, clapping and cheering. Eventually, laughing uncontrollably,* NELSON *and* EMMA *come to a stop and, supporting each other, stagger towards the champagne.* LADY NELSON, *pulling herself together, confronts them.*

LADY NELSON. Horatio: I am resolved –

NELSON. This is entirely ridiculous –

LADY NELSON. If you will not give her up, then –

NELSON. You have no dignity, Lady Nelson –

LADY NELSON. Then you will have to give up me.

This exchange has fallen into a pool of embarrassed general silence.

REBIRTH THROUGH THE FLAMES:

PRINCE. Dammit, this is personal, it's confoundedly private, dammit, and altogether out of place. I am going to propose a toast.

NELSON. And what about my own dignity? It is clear you have no purpose but to take all pains to diminish it.

PRINCE. My lord, I said a toast. The King, God bless him.

ALL. The King, God bless him.

PRINCE. I am going to propose another toast. To the Victor of the Nile.

ALL. The Victor of the Nile.

PRINCE. I haven't finished yet. To the Victor of the Nile and also to his good lady – who appears to be about to leave us. Dear lady, I protest that your absence at this moment would be most hurtful to my feelings.

LADY NELSON. I cannot run counter to the express desire of Your Royal Highness.

PRINCE. Splendid, splendid, splendid. Flagons. Bumpers. Brimmers. Death to the French. Confusion to that Bonaparte. Damnation to Republicans. Republicans – reminds me – yes – what the devil did you mean, Hamilton, by describing that damn diadem as a *republican* trophy?

HAMILTON. Oh, why, Your Royal Highness, it was only –

PRINCE. Castrated antiquarianism, sir: and the ruin of this country! You've been getting it out of a book. Scribble scribble scribble – it's all you ever find time to do! You're no better than the Frogs. All those books they wrote in France and we know what happened there. Now the rot has spread to England. I took occasion, just a few minutes ago, to wander round the library in there – and by Gad sir, I found this!

He holds out a tipsy GIRL *who is holding a book, which the* PRINCE *in turn holds up and thrusts under the nose of his* HOST.

Voltaire, by all that's treasonable! Anti-church, anti-monarchy, and anti-good-morality! Come come sir, have you more of them?

HOST. Oh Good God yes, shelves of them!

PRINCE. And if it hadn't been for Lord Nelson and his gallant
tars upon the sea, you'd have had a housefull, I suppose?
Deeds, d'you see, deeds, none of your confounded words:
and only by means of unquestioning deeds can we achieve
a sound morality!

One of the GUESTS *laughs. The* PRINCE *turns on him in a fury.*

Sound morality. Sound morality. If any man has any doubts
of it, Lord Nelson will set them right. Set them right, my
lord, set them right at once!

NELSON. Morality, Your Royal Highness. . . . My own father
is a clergyman. . . .

PRINCE. Exactly so: and you have proven it, my lord, to the
last drop of your blood! Now: you sir, *you* must prove it.
All this filthy kind of nonsense on your shelves – and you
invite your Prince into the building! Don't you think you
ought to burn them?

HOST. But sir, they are my property –

PRINCE. A gentleman's allegiance is of more import than his
property! So burn them: burn them *now!*

HOST. I admit it, I confess it, Lord Nelson's example puts us
all to shame!

(*He sings.*)

> He puts us all to shame with his deeds and daring
> We vegetate at home when the war we should be
>   sharing,
> Our spirit and our mind are both degenerated,
> Our eyes are all but blind, our pipes are constipated,
> Full of pen-and-ink, the more we sit and think,
> The more we only blink, instead of up and raging.
> A book is no damn good – I'll tell you what we need –
> We need a glorious deed – so set them all a-blazing!

All the GUESTS *are dancing to his song and now they join in the
chorus with ferocious emphasis –*

GUESTS (*sing*).
> One two three four five, pile 'em up and Burn 'em
> Heave 'em in the fire and set them all a-blazing –
> Whack fol lol de ra!

PRINCE. So fetch in a brazier – so fetch in all the books –
HOST. Shelves thirteen to seventeen – clear them off and bring them in –

PRINCE, HOST *and* GUESTS *roar off to collect the books.*

HAMILTON. Drunk: they are all drunk.
NELSON. Yet I suppose one could say that their hearts are in the right place. Even civilian nincompoops are not inevitably to be despised –

(*He sings.*)

> When we admit we are at fault, when barnacles and weed
> Do clog the planking of our craft and drag at our proper speed –
> Then surely we should take the time –

LADY NELSON (*singing, aggressively and pointedly*).
> – and take the time again
> Above and below the waterline to scrape and holystone!

NELSON. Fanny – I beseech you!
FANNY (*sings*).
> My husband dear, it is too late for you to understand.
> He underwent his overhaul before ever he reached this land:
> He is a new man now indeed, both mast and rigging and keel,
> And I'd rather far that he lay drowned in the waters of the Nile.

Thank heaven we have no children.

The book-burners now charge in again, carrying armfuls of books. One of them holds a brazier. They are all shouting the names of various obnoxious authors – e.g.: Voltaire, Rousseau, Blake, Coleridge, Wordsworth, Diderot, etc.

HOST (*sings*).

> Your Rousseau and Voltaire are scarcely worth the
>   paper –
> Scatter them and tear, and every other faker
> Who'd turn your brain to mud, your will to milk and
>   water,
> You'd watch without a word a man who'd rape your
>   daughter,
> Shoot and kill your dad, hit you on the head,
> Shed your mother's blood with cruelty amazing:
> So, leave them no excuse, your culture you must lose,
> It's nothing but abuse: so set it all a-blazing!

GUESTS (*in chorus as they dance round the brazier destroying
the books*).

> One two three four five, pile 'em and burn 'em,
> Heave 'em in the fire and set them all a-blazing!
> Whack fol lol de ra!

EMMA (*sings*).

> I did not want to do it but by God it has been done:
> He must declare himself for me before all this roaring
>   room.
> He stands and stammers on one leg and then on the
>   other he turns
> While the mildewed ancient history in the brazier
>   crackles and burns.
> My lord, you must attend to me and you must attend
>   to her:
> She put to you a question and you answered never a
>   word:
> It is her or me: which will you have – ?

LADY NELSON (*sings*).

> I am waiting for a reply.

NELSON (*sings*).

> I will love my Lady Hamilton until the day I die.

EMMA. So he's said it.

LADY NELSON. Yes, he's said it.

NELSON. I didn't mean to –

EMMA AND ⎫
LADY NELSON⎰ Yes he did. Yes you did.

PRINCE (*at the brazier*). Thomas Paine! 'The Rights of Man'
... Good God he was an Englishman – I burn him per-
sonally, Goddammit!

HAMILTON. Did what? What is happening? Any man that
can burn books must be an absolute madman.

*The book-burning party has now declined into a circle of help-
lessly drunk people dancing arm in arm around the fire like Red
Indians.*

EMMA (*sings*).
    The time has come for every man
    To run most raving mad
    The time has come for every man,
    To throw away his head –
The tumbrils, the guillotine, we all need the rattle and the
thump of the quick clean guillotine –

(*She sings.*)
    But for every man that's murdered
    Another must be born
    Whether he comes as a naked babe
    Or a full-grown god of war.

HAMILTON. To bring forth full-grown gods of war, my dear,
you must first impregnate the good earth with poisoned
dragons' teeth.

The book-burners, with a final roar, surge off the stage and out.
HAMILTON *grabs hold of* MRS CADOGAN.

    Dear Lady, I have your cloak ...

He takes MRS CADOGAN *out.* EMMA *and* NELSON *are alone
in one corner,* LADY NELSON *and* NISBET *in another.*

EMMA. Dangerous or not, you will never grow anything if the
furrow is not fertile.
NELSON. Fertile?
EMMA. The Good Earth was always held to be the greatest of

goddesses: when she couples with an equally potent divinity, the conception is gigantic. Mars?

NELSON. Venus?

EMMA. Oh my sweet and tortured lover, I am with child.

NELSON. This cannot be true.

EMMA. I swear to you it is.

NELSON. We must trumpet it abroad like the tidings of the Nile.

EMMA. No.

NELSON.

> I am bewildered and confused
> I have had too much champagne –
> A gale is rising out at sea –
> Who can tell the weather-vane?
> From the north or from the south
> I cannot tell it clear
> But it brings the black reek over me –
> The flag is on fire
> And the long guns they do roar . . .

EMMA.

> You have had too much champagne . . .

NELSON.

> I am bewildered and confused
> Alas for my poor Fanny –

EMMA.

> She has been terribly abused . . .

NELSON. No, no, the weather-vane. . . . Hardy, where is the weather-vane. . . . Hardy – ?

He staggers out, with his arm hooked round EMMA'*s hips and his head tucked underneath her breast.* ALLEN *follows with the cocked hat.*

LADY NELSON. And his arm was blown away and his eye was beaten out, and he was so ill he could not stand, yet he still went off to sea and still he came back again. Always I knew that one voyage he would not come back. How was I to know that a man can be drowned and yet still he can sail home?

NISBET *makes an effort at sobriety and leads his mother away,
tripping over his own feet.*

THE HERO ENDEAVOURS TO RECOLLECT HIMSELF:

NELSON *enters and wanders confusedly around among a collection of half-unpacked furniture and luggage, which is being
brought in by* SAILORS.
ALLEN *comes in and out with more luggage, adding to the confusion, and takes no notice of* NELSON, *who is in an intro-
spective mood and in turn takes no notice of him. After a while*
ALLEN *stops working and turns to the audience.*

ALLEN. I've never known him in such confusion in all my
   life – but you can't be surprised at it, can you, considering
   what's happened?

(*He sings.*)

> They fetched him home and half-disgraced him,
> Said he was not fit to fight:
> England's great reputation foundered
> In a strumpet's cunt so tight.
>
> But the war goes on regardless –
> Why should Boney give a damn
> For the long joyful painful torment
> Of our leading married man?
>
> We all have wives, we all have sweethearts,
> We don't all treat them very well:
> But we must arise and leave them
> When the press-gang's on the prowl.

SEAMEN, *enforced by the Press-gang, stumble resentfully up the
gangplank onto the ship. One man is torn in a classical fashion
from the arms of his wife.*

SEAMAN'S WIFE (*sings*).
> It's oh the weary cutters,

> They ha' taen my love frae me
> It's oh the weary cutters
> They ha' taen my love frae me:
> They've shipped him awa' foreign wi' Nelson
> Beyond the salt sea –
> It's oh the weary cutters,
> They ha' taen my love frae me . . .

BOSUN. All women off the ship – come on, get them women off the ship – no use at all for you to keep on squalling on the gangway, love: if he comes home, he comes home – if he don't, he'll be drowned – come on now, clear the decks of all them lovely women – !

ALLEN. More of a formality, really – there's usually a few dozen manage to slip aboard and stay aboard. Always the fattest, oddly enough. I'd better go and sort him out. After all, he *is* an Admiral . . .

He places himself in NELSON's *path and tugs his forelock.*

NELSON (*becoming aware of his surroundings*). This is a disgraceful sight, Allen. Why is nothing unpacked yet?

ALLEN. Beg your pardon, milord: there seems to have been a bit of a confusion. Lady Nelson insisted on packing everything herself.

NELSON. Lady Nelson? So I get the wrong clothes, the wrong furniture, the wrong everything, I suppose. I will write to Lady Nelson:

> I will write and put an end
> To fifteen years of cordial marriage
> With a bad-tempered letter
> About badly-packed luggage.

ALLEN. On the subject of letters, milord –

NELSON. Yes, yes, letters – what!

ALLEN. No, milord, it's not for you. It's addressed care-of you, in a manner of speaking, to somebody of the name of Thompson.

NELSON. Will you give it to me at once!

ALLEN. Was you about to appoint some officer of that name, sir, for if so, then perhaps –

NELSON. Yes yes, Lieutenant Thompson, or Warrant Officer
  Thompson, or Thompson the Master Gunner or Thompson
  the Carpenter's Mate – or Admiral Thompson . . . give it
  here and get out!

ALLEN. Aye aye, sir – here you are, sir.

He gives NELSON *the letter and goes.*

NELSON. Thompson is an Admiral: what else could he be?
  What, so Lord Nelson is afraid – Lord Nelson once again
  about to fly his flag against the French?
      Yes of course he is afraid.
      By this time she might have died.

He tears open the letter, and reads it wildly to himself.

      By this time she has a child.
      By this time she has a daughter.
      By this time *I* have a daughter.
      Born with a false name
      In a false and secret corner
      And *I* must fly my flag once more
      Wide agape on the open water . . .
      Horatia Nelson Thompson
      That is the lie by which we must call her:
      She has a liar for a father
      And a liar for a mother –
      What lies will lie before her
      As she walks into a world
      Where all true men are defeated
      By the falsehood of treacherous murder
      And false men are accepted
      With all the credit of the conqueror?
      But I must write a letter to my Angel,
      I can find neither pen nor pencil:
      'O my dearest dearest Emma – !'

He starts feverishly to write and then recollects himself.

  'Emma' – not at all, not at all. 'To Mrs Emma Nelson
  Thompson' – this is not to Mrs Thompson, it is a letter
  about Mrs Thompson.

'To Lady Hamilton: I believe Mrs Thompson's friend will
go mad with joy. . . .' And so I will, by God. 'He cries,
prays, and performs all tricks, yet dare not shew his feelings,
but he has only me to consult with.' Now look here, Thompson, will you put yourself in frame? What do you want me
to write to your wife? Oh, she's not even your wife, is she,
she's not even called Thompson, let alone *Mrs*? So you
got her into trouble, did you, Thompson? Could she not
marry you? I hope you want to marry her, Thompson, you
can't play fast and loose, you know, not on my ship – I
inculcate a sound Christian morality among my seamen, I
would have you know, sir. My own father is a clergyman
and –

> Goddammit, once again
> I have a shooting pain
> In the wrist of my right hand.
> This is to me a clear sign
> That death is not the end.
> The immortality of the soul
> By this paradoxical pain
> To me is made most plain.
> Thus we find the uttermost truths of religion
> Confirmed most convincingly by an adulterer's ampu-
>   tation.

I cannot write: so I will say so, and kiss the paper and send
it off.

He finishes the letter distractedly.
Enter ALLEN.

ALLEN. Oh – milord –
NELSON. Post this letter. Bring champagne.
ALLEN. Whatever you say, milord.

He fetches the champagne.

NELSON. Oh you are to have some too.
ALLEN. Milord?
NELSON. Oh yes, you are to drink to Mrs Thompson's health.
ALLEN. Mrs Thompson's –

NELSON. She's a relative of mine – or something – a very good lady. Drink her health, man, drink her health. She's just had a baby.

ALLEN. Oh yes, milord. Very pleased, milord. Congratulations.

NELSON. Not me, you jackass. Thompson.

ALLEN. Yes, milord, of course, milord – I meant, in absence-like – congratulations.

NELSON (*raising his glass*). Mrs Thompson.

ALLEN (*drinking*). Mrs Thompson's health, milord.

NELSON. And another one: Mrs Thompson.

They drink again, NELSON *sings.*

> And another one: Mrs Thompson!
> Do you not know Mrs Thompson?
> If you don't know Mrs Thompson
> You're nothing but a blockhead!

ALLEN (*sings*).

> Mrs Thompson's health, milord.
> I'm sure we're all both glad and proud
> But I'm warning you they're both aboard
> With gold-lace on their cocked-hats!

NELSON (*he sings*).

> Who's aboard – the mother and baby?

ALLEN (*he sings*).

> No, milord, but the regular navy –
> Admirals both, and Captain Hardy
> Don't know what to do, sir.

Enter ST VINCENT *and* PARKER. ALLEN *discreetly goes out.*

ST VINCENT (*sings*).

> My lord, on board is Lord St Vincent
> With Admiral Parker in attendance:
> We want to see you at this instant –

NELSON (*singing and thrusting drinks at them*).

> Here's a glass for *you*, sir!
> You must drink the health of Mrs Thompson
> I will pour you a drink for Mrs Thompson:

Don't stand there in such confusion –
I desire to play the host, sir!

PARKER (*sings*).

But we're under orders for Copenhagen.

NELSON (*sings*).

Are we? Yes, of course, I've read 'em –
Has something happened to delay them?
Why don't you drink my toast, sir?

ST VINCENT } Oh very well then – Mrs Thompson.
AND PARKER }

ST VINCENT. This is highly hospitable of you, Nelson: do you intend to continue tippling all the way to the Baltic?

NELSON. Please excuse me, my lord – I have not yet obtained a grip of my surroundings – but I trust I do appreciate the main point of my being here.

PARKER. Which is?

NELSON. To destroy the Danish fleet.

ST VINCENT. Indeed no it is not. Your orders are to prevent the government of Denmark handing over its fleet to the French.

PARKER. Not at all the same thing. Denmark, recollect, is neutral.

NELSON. As was Naples?

PARKER. Ah, you recollect *that*?

THE BLIND EYE:

ST VINCENT. He means, and by God he's your superior officer on this venture, Nelson, you must listen to him with both ears – he means that we don't fire the cannon in Copenhagen until letters have been written and conversations have been held. Admiral Parker will converse: you, if you please, will wait in patience till he's done so.

NELSON. And when he *has* done so?

ST VINCENT. In all probability, then, you must destroy the Danish fleet. . . . Excellent: so I'll waste no more of your time. You will have much to attend to before you set sail, I make no doubt. Set about it: and good luck.

NELSON. Thank you, my lord.

Exit NELSON.

ST VINCENT. Parker, he's your man: control him: don't lose him.

PARKER. Don't want him. Unreliable. Shan't have him.

ST VINCENT. Must have him. He'll win the war for you.

PARKER. Just because he disobeyed you once, and got away with it, you seem to think he is a genius.

ST VINCENT. Don't you? Supposing the Danes refuse to accept your diplomatic overtures. You will have to attack them. They are anchored in their harbour. They are heavily armed. You might as well be attacking a line of ramparted fortresses. You will need courage, endurance, rapidity of decision, total confidence in the men under your command, and a complete disregard of casualties. The casualties will be enormous.

> They will have to be accounted for,
> By somebody, to Parliament –
> What better man than Nelson
> To take the blame and bear the brunt?
> Good God, sir, we do him a good turn,
> If you look at it right –
> Of course nobody would mind at all
> If she wasn't a wedded wife . . .

Exit ST VINCENT. PARKER *takes his stand on one side of the stage.* NELSON *and* HARDY *enter and stand at the other.*

PARKER. Letters have been written: conversations have been held. Diplomatic overtures have been entirely unsuccessful. I am therefore reluctantly committed to the destruction of the Danish fleet.

NELSON. When?

PARKER. Not just yet. We must wait until –

NELSON. Why?

PARKER. Never mind why. I give the orders, dammit.

NELSON. We'll miss the tide. There's a lot of shoal water.

PARKER. I too am well equipped with charts.

NELSON. I know where I'm going to put my ships. I know every depth to a fraction of a fathom. Hardy has been out all night in a ship's boat taking soundings. Why the devil can't we attack?

PARKER. Not safe.

NELSON. Coward.

PARKER. Sir!

NELSON. Ha ha I've hurt his honour. But he is, you know, isn't he, Hardy?

HARDY. Not for me to say, sir.

PARKER. It's nothing whatever to do with courage. It's politics. I am terrified of politics.

NELSON. Coward. A government's to be fought against, just the same as any Frenchman. *I'm* not afraid of it.

PARKER. On *your* head then. So I give the order. Make the signal for close action. And I only got married last month. Oh my poor wife, whatever shall I say to you if they put me on the beach?

NELSON. So we go in and drop anchor, ship against ship and we pound them till they can't take it. It's going to last all day and the Danskers can replace dead men from the shore. We can't, of course, and they're knocking us down like skittles.

PARKER. He'll never get out of it. Good God, there's his top-mast gone. Gracious heaven he's on fire.

NELSON. No I'm not.

PARKER. Well it looks like it from here. Tell that raving lunatic to break off the action at once – God if I had St Vincent here I would strangle him with my own hands – you don't suppose he's drunk? I mean Nelson, is he drunk?

The signal to break off action is hoisted.

HARDY. Signal from the flagship to break off action at once, sir.

NELSON. Yes. I can't see it.

HARDY. Take my glass, sir.

NELSON. Idiot.

HARDY. But you can't just ignore it –

NELSON. Hardy, you're a blockhead. An old and dear friend
but an absolute blockhead. Where's one of the boys?
Youngster, just come here a moment.

He supports his telescope on the ship's-boy's shoulder.

Captain Hardy, you will observe, please, that I am looking
at the flagship through a large telescope properly supported
and I am none the less unable to distinguish the Admiral's
signal. That's in case of a court-martial. There is, you will
testify, a very great deal of smoke.

HARDY. There's also a white flag.

NELSON. What! Oho, I see *that* all right! The Danskers have
capitulated. God: I knew that I could do it.

He closes his telescope with a snap and walks over to PARKER.

All it needs is application. You could have done just as well
yourself.

PARKER.
            Oh yes, it's your victory:
            Don't think I feel jealousy.
            But Denmark was no enemy
            Until we opened fire upon their fleet.
            This is not, in my opinion
            The way we ought to treat
            Every wavering frightened nation
            That is threatened by Bonaparte.
            He can never win their heart:
            Why should we destroy their people?
            It was just the same at Naples.

NELSON.
            Destruction must continue until Bonaparte is dead!
            Napoleon Bonaparte is *not yet dead!*
            I could have killed him once and I will do it before I
                die.
            But for the matter of Naples, I refuse to apologize:
            My conduct in that city was tactically wise,
            Personally heroic, and strategically justified:
            I look back on it with pride.

PARKER. We turn the world into a wilderness and we have the
   nerve to call it peace.

NELSON. Shakespeare?

PARKER. Tacitus. But he was not an Admiral.

*Exeunt. Dead and wounded seamen are carried across the stage,
groans and cries and screams.*

PEACE: AS CREATED BY THE TREATY OF AMIENS, 1802.

Enter NISBET.

NISBET. Yet even as the result of this kind of a shambles
   we do occasionally find ourselves at peace . . .

Act Three

Enter NISBET, *in his uniform, but carrying a civilian coat.*

NISBET. We do occasionally find ourselves at peace. No particular reason: but a whole decade of war: and the participants are exhausted.

(*He sings.*)

> The bare-arsed hordes of hungry Frenchmen
> Stand exactly as they were:
> The Kings of Europe have not destroyed them,
> The Poor of Europe are just as poor.
>
> The crowned Kings of Royal Europe
> Still sit proudly on their thrones:
> The furious French have not destroyed them,
> The furious French have a King of their own.
>
> They did not want him nor expect him,
> They do not know yet that he is there:
> They know he is a successful general,
> They know he has not lost the war.
>
> But I've lost mine and I feel no guilt for it,
> The blue and the gold I do discard –

He takes off his officer's coat and puts on the other one.

> If I were a gaudy and jingling hero
> I would no doubt take it very hard . . .'

Enter HARDY (*in uniform*).

Captain Hardy?

HARDY. Captain Nisbet?

NISBET. Oh Mister Nisbet, I think. . . . I have set myself up in business, you see, and I am happy to tell you I look like making a great deal of money. Are you on your way to visit him?

HARDY. If you are referring to Lord Nelson –

NISBET. I am. Have you been to see his wife?

HARDY. Wife . . . ?

NISBET. Not Hamilton's wife – *his*! She lives in Bath, in retirement, and is very lonely and unhappy. I said: have you been to see her?

HARDY. I had hopes that I would be able – soon – er – as a matter of fact – no.

NISBET. No: of course not. Now that the war is over, preferment in the service is of necessity difficult, for no senior officers are getting themselves killed. So Captain Hardy should pay no visits that might upset his ancient friendship with our most famous living Admiral.

HARDY. If you continue in this offensive manner, young man, I shall be compelled to demand satisfaction from you!

NISBET. I don't want *your* satisfaction, Captain Hardy: but I do want it from *him*. Would you please give him this?

He hands HARDY *a letter.*

HARDY. It is a challenge?

NISBET. Yes indeed: but not from me.

HARDY. This is Lady Nelson's handwriting . . .

REMEMBRANCE OF GREAT AFFECTION:

LADY NELSON (*singing, above and off*).
    He is the hero of this land
    For all the battles he has won
    He gave his health and strength away
    And asked but one thing in return.

NISBET. Oh nothing very much he wanted – just a woman that didn't belong to him.

LADY NELSON (*singing*).

> He is the hero of my heart
> For all the love I bore to him
> I gave my health and strength away
> And ask but one thing in return.

NISBET. And she asks it for the last time. She will never write to him again if he does not choose to answer. Oh it's nothing very much that she's wanting – just –

LADY NELSON. – Just the company of my dear husband in a comfortable warm house that I would be able to make ready. . . . Do let us live together once more. I can never be happy until such an event takes place.

NISBET. I advised her not to write it: but she would. She wants him back.

HARDY. She demanded that he chose between her and – and the other one: and he did make his choice. I do not see how –

NISBET. She deferred to his greatness, Captain Hardy, for she knew that he was great. If he reads this letter he will know that she is feeble: and she hopes, she feebly hopes, that he will recognize her weakness, and defer to it, in his turn. . . . You will give him the letter?

HARDY. I can hardly refuse. But –

NISBET. Thank you.

He turns to go: and then stops.

Oh, by the way – is it true that La Belle Hamilton has dropped one?

HARDY. Dropped – ?

NISBET. A brat, a bundle, an unexpected handful – ? Don't look so startled: it may not be anything more than a malicious fabrication.

(*He sings.*)

> Oh who's the father of your child?
> Ho-ho me dearie duckie – oh –
> I found him in the ocean wild
> A-floating in a bucket – oh.

Exit NISBET.

HARDY. I make it a point of honour to hear none of these calumnies: and if I do hear them, I don't believe them. I only believe what I see. I have seen St Vincent, I have seen the Nile, I have seen Copenhagen: and what is worth far more than all of these, I have seen British Jack Tars putting their lives in hazard, willingly, without fear of the Frenchmen and without fear of the cat-o-nine-tails. It is not long since the entire Home Fleet was in a state of rabid mutiny. Nelson's crews were unaffected – why? Because his men were well aware that he was well aware of their justified grievances: and he trusted them to trust him: and they did. They were not driven to their duty: and when they died, they gave three cheers for King George. You may ask: to what purpose? Well: the war is over, is it not? Surely, in that, there is answer enough.

Enter MRS CADOGAN.

MRS CADOGAN. And here he is, God bless him, the long-awaited guest! Captain Hardy: welcome to Merton, sir: oh how delighted Lord Nelson and my Emma and poor old William are about to be directly, to see you once again as large as life and in their very midst – go right along in to the house, sir: and very welcome you will be made, I'm sure.

HARDY. Thank you, Mrs Cadogan, I will do precisely that. What beautiful weather we are having, are we not? But alas, the news from Europe – ominous, ma'am, wouldn't you say? Bonaparte, Bonaparte ... the cursèd nuisance won't stay quiet ... tut tut tut ...

Exit HARDY.

MRS CADOGAN.
> His friends and his relatives
> Continue to call
> Quite thronging us out
> In the parlour and hall

And sprawling all over
On chair and on sofa
Round the dining room table
They're a regular rabble –
Sir William doesn't take to them one little bit, I am sorry
to say: and as for this poor innocent –

*She hauls the baby from out of a dark corner – toys and blankets
are spilling off in confusion.*

– there is nothing we can do with her but pack her back
again to London where the nurse is in receipt of a regular
weekly stipend plus a perfectly ruinous bonus on account
of the secrecy . . .

EMMA *and* NELSON *enter. He wears a black civilian coat and
carries his medals.*

NELSON.
        My darling, it does not fit.
EMMA.
        It was bought for you by Tom Tit.
NELSON.
        With the medals it will look absurd.
EMMA.
        Then do not wear them:
        We are not observed.
        We are entirely on our own –
NELSON.
        – Except for Sir William –
EMMA.
        In our private country home.
        It is not in fact necessary
        For you to wear anything at all.
NELSON.
        My friends and my relatives
        Will continue to call.
        I must shew myself decorous
        And aware of my position.

EMMA.

But you have no position:
For there is no war.
You need to be nothing more
Than what in fact you are.
So, my love, put these away,
And let us both together pray
That never never never
Will you need them again.

NELSON.

Because we see the bright and shining sun
We are in error if we dream
That God has finished with the rain.

EMMA.

God?

NELSON.

The French say Destiny.
I prefer to call it villainy.
This treaty has no meaning
For nobody has won.

MRS CADOGAN *comes forward with the baby.*

Enjoy your little daughter
To the full extent of pleasure
I doubt if we shall have leisure
To provide you with a son.
Come on come on come on this is completely ridiculous –
It's a beautiful morning
We have nothing to do with it but play in the garden.
How very kind of Mrs Thompson
To bring her baby to see us –

MRS CADOGAN.

I'm afraid that she's teething
She's inclined to be fractious –

NELSON.

Congenital, inherited
And who gives a damn for it?

Dear Emma, I am positive
This coat does not fit.

NELSON *and* EMMA *go out.*
MRS CADOGAN, *left alone, croons consolingly to the baby.*

MRS CADOGAN (*sings*).
Never mind never mind
Oh my pretty little monkey
One day you will be told
And one day you will find
What sort of proud glory
You had for your daddy
What sort of laughing lady
Was your gay and careless mammy . . .

She is interrupted by a bacchanalian burst of laughter from offstage.

THE HERO'S HAPPY HOME:

She takes the baby out and immediately returns without her. One of the child's toys has been left unnoticed on the floor.
MRS CADOGAN. There, now: that's got rid of her – out of sight, the little precious – out of sight and all is safe: though by no means out of mind.

More convivial roaring. NELSON *and* EMMA *enter with* NELSON's RELATIVES – *an indeterminate number – say two men, two women. One of them is* NELSON's *old father, the clergyman – he is very senile and perhaps in a wheelchair – the others are youngish and bold and noisy.* ALLEN *trundles in a table loaded with food and they all crowd around it and guzzle.*

NELSON. Has anyone seen the newspapers today?
RELATIVES. Surely you don't get the newspapers every day down here in the country, Horace – ? Damn the newspapers, I say – nothing but rumours and deliberate attempts to frighten us – nonsense to suppose that the French can be

meaning to try anything now – Good God they had their
licking before – yes, Horace saw to that, did you not,
Horace ? – they wouldn't dare – they wouldn't dare – oho
would they not, though ? Stick your hand up Boney's arse
and he will shit in your fist! – Port or Madeira, father ?
Madeira for me – d'you hear, Allen, Madeira – what –
what – ? Father wants to know, Horace, if the war begins
again – will you be given a command ?

NELSON. If the war begins again ? Not a question of *if*. What
you should say is *when*.

EMMA. Will you have another partridge – Allen, pay attention –
the partridges are to be served! *I* have got a newspaper –
there is nothing in it about war.

NELSON. Let me see it.

EMMA. No – Horace – wait a moment. There is nothing in it
about war.

A RELATIVE. No more there is neither. Bread riots in Manchester.

RELATIVES. There are always riots in Manchester – why don't
they send in the dragoons – ? Rick-burnings in Dorset –
workmens' combinations broken up in West Hampshire by
the county constable and his men – presumed Jacobins
under surveillance in the suburbs of Sheffield – nothing at
all about the war.

NELSON. Will you let me see that newspaper!

RELATIVES (*singing*).

> There is nothing at all as we sit round this board
> To make us confused or annoyed or disturbed:
> We fill our good bellies with food and good wine
> Our funds are invested and interest will gain.
>> Our interest will gain
>> And our trade will increase
>> We feed and we fatten
>> Whatever will happen
> John Bull he has conquered, John Bull is at peace.

NELSON *has now at last obtained the paper and is hunting
rapidly through it.*

NELSON. Now wait a moment – Emma – the newspaper – all
the pages are not here – all the foreign news has been
removed – someone has been deliberately concealing the
pages of this newspaper –

*His voice has risen to an alarmingly high pitch and the greedy
roar of the* RELATIVES *breaks off short with embarrassment.*

ALLEN. I don't know nothing about it, my lord. I'll go in and
hunt them up. It could be they've got left in the . . .

He goes out hurriedly.

NELSON. It is not I that want to go to war! And if I must go –
I go only as the servant of my King. But Bonaparte – consider Bonaparte – he has no choice in the matter at all
– his entire reputation depends upon the successful
organization of slaughter –
RELATIVES. So does yours, dear Horace – so does yours –
NELSON. No!

(*He sings.*)

        By gun and by gunshot
        Alone he made his name.
EMMA (*sings*).
        Yet we hear them say of Nelson
        Exactly the same.
NELSON (*sings*).
        When there is no fighting
        He becomes a withered root.
EMMA (*sings*).
        A mandrake pulled out
        To scream and to shout.
NELSON (*sings*).
        They all will look at him and wonder
        Whatever did he do?
EMMA (*sings*).
        This naked thing so thin and pale
        His hair so gray, his teeth so few – ?

NELSON (*sings*).
     To restore to the bold Napoleon –
EMMA (*sings*).
     To restore to the bold Nelson –
EMMA *and* NELSON (*sing*).
     The triumph of his power –
NELSON (*sings*).
     Is to bring back to all Frenchmen –
EMMA (*sings*).
     Is to bring back to Englishmen –
EMMA *and* NELSON (*sing*).
     Both bloody death and fear.

The RELATIVES, *not quite getting the point, applaud and beat their fists on the table.* EMMA *and* NELSON *are confronting one another tensely, some distance away from the crowd.*

NELSON. I do not think we are at one, my dear. No no, we are discordant.

A BIRD UPON A PERCH:

Enter HAMILTON *in a dressing-gown, looking decrepit.*

HAMILTON. Please leave my house. You are making far too much noise and have continued to do so for seventeen days. Lady Hamilton has borne with you in patience and so has Lord Nelson: but I am not at all well and I would be glad if you would go.
EMMA. He's quite right. He is not well. I think you had better go.

NELSON *makes a helpless gesture.*

RELATIVES. Well, really, whose house is it? I mean, who is married to whom? We never had this sort of nonsense when we used to go and stay with Fanny – Fanny knew how to entertain her guests – after all we're not just any-body, we are the family, Goddammit . . . *etc.*

The RELATIVES *retire, grumbling – the old clergyman singing gaily in his wheelchair.*

HAMILTON. Mrs Cadogan, you may stay, of course – you are a good quiet soul and inoffensive about the premises. And I also make an exception in the case of Captain Hardy, who –

NELSON. Hardy – is he here?

HAMILTON. He came upstairs to see me – he said he would not join the company until the noise was somewhat abated. A most sensible gentleman.

He sees the toy and picks it up.

So so – what have we here?
> A wooden bird upon a perch
> Painted feathers blue and gray:
> I think he wants to fly away.
> I think I want to fly away –
> But where to go I cannot tell.
> The heroes of the ancient world
> Would dream of the meads of asphodel –

Do you know what asphodel is? Most disappointing – a spikey little plant of no particular beauty, doesn't smell of anything very much, you can't eat it – but nevertheless there is this time-honoured picture of the Elysian fields – strong perfect golden naked bodies stretched out on the hillside in the clear transparent Mediterranean warmth –

(*He sings.*)

> Male and female there they lie
> Sometimes apart sometimes entwined
> They do not itch nor stink of sweat
> Their lips and loins are sweet and clean.
>
> They do not hiccup when they eat
> They do not grunt when they make love
> Their hands and eyes without disdain
> So freely from one to the other may rove.

Exactly the kind of improbable freedom that the French

lately thought they could re-create, I believe. But all they made was Bonaparte – and here in the newspaper we can read what he is doing.

He has a page of the paper.

NELSON. Where did you find that! I mean – er – what *is* he doing?

HAMILTON. He is making himself Emperor. Icarus or Phaëton, does the fellow think he is ? He will scale the heights of heaven!

He plays with the toy, discovering that its wings flap when a little knob is turned. He sings.

> You turn the knob, the wings will flap
> The flesh will tremble, the heart will move:
> My heart is dying but I saw to my joy
> That yours were alive and alive with love.

And I did think that I could share in it. I have not been disappointed but, alas, we can compel the situation too far.

(*He sings.*)

> We have each one thing we cannot share
> He lives deep down inside and dark:
> A leaping puppet on a string
> Unique and private Bonaparte.
>
> He plays tom-fool with a bloodstained sword
> He tries to jump out of our mouth
> And once he's out we are destroyed
> The whole world knows what we are about.

He gives way to a burst of coughing.

I nearly brought him up, didn't I ? Horrid, black, malodorous, bilious creature – enough to frighten a child into fits. What child, by the way ? For whom is this pretty bird intended ?

EMMA (*after a pause*). Mrs Thompson's baby.

HAMILTON. Mrs Thompson ? Oh dear . . . I suppose I should

not ask you for any fuller answer. (*He coughs again.*) I can't keep him down, you know. God protect *you*, my lord, from such bronchial mortification. Do you know that my Emma was *sold* to me once? By my own nephew, what is more.

EMMA. Oh no – we don't talk about that –

HAMILTON. Yes. Sold. And the price that I paid for her was to make my nephew my sole heir. Which means that when I shortly afterwards decided to marry her, I did so in the knowledge that she was already disinherited. I was very wrong to do this.

NELSON. Sir William, Emma has told me about all this – you must not feel guilty for it – what was done was done and –

MRS CADOGAN. But there's more to it, though – isn't there – I mean she's that fat and soaked with gin that I couldn't dispose of her to nobody now: so when *he* dies, which won't be long, who's going to keep her? *You* – with all them greedyguts of relatives what we've just this minute shewn the door to? And then what if there *is* another war and you go off to it and die?

NELSON } (*together*). Mrs Cadogan, please restrain your tongue – how can you talk like that!

EMMA } Why can't you keep your trap shut, you stupid old bitch!

MRS CADOGAN. Oh well, if that's your attitude . . .

She goes out in dudgeon.

HAMILTON. Mrs Cadogan is perfectly correct – even to the matter of the gin. Is she not, Emma?

EMMA. Christ then, who drove me to it?

HAMILTON. My nephew, you know, recommended her to me on the ground that she was the sweetest-smelling bed-fellow that anyone could wish for. You see, it is all self-deception – it is all of a piece with the Elysian Asphodel.

On the day of my death
She will be left with her bad breath.

And she'll expend even that upon some undeserving low companion. There is no other woman in this world of such extravagant generosity. I can never forgive myself. Lord Nelson: you have been very bold with my Emma. You have paraded her upside down before the astonished public gaze, with your arses across the yardarm and your foreheads on the deck. What, do you imagine the rules of marriage are as easily subverted as the hidebound traditions of the fleet? So you see what you have come to.

> You are left, upon my death
> With her and her bad breath.
> What will she do, tomorrow?
> Will she steal, or will she borrow?
> Or else, will you, with your great reputation –

NELSON.

> Demand her upkeep from a grateful nation!

HAMILTON.

> You take the words out of my mouth.

NELSON.

> I know what I am about.
> The services which she has wrought
> For love of me, for all this land,
> *By* all this land with open hand
> Shall be rewarded in abundant measure!
> I will inform the people: they will pour out their treasure.

HAMILTON. They will: they must: by heaven you must promise me they shall!

EMMA. But will they listen? The hero will then be dead. Who will believe what a dead man has to say?

HAMILTON.

> The people love this dead man and they love his whore
> As much as all his courage or even more . . .

My dear, you are notorious: you are exactly what the public imagination delights in. Shall I shew you an example? Mr Allen, please come here!

Enter ALLEN.

Now, Mr Allen: here is a guinea for you, if you will
answer me frankly a very simple question I am about to
put to you.

ALLEN. Thank you sir: very happy, sir.

HAMILTON. How many wives is a sailor expected to have?

ALLEN. A wife in every port, sir.

HAMILTON. Exactly so. *Vox populi*. You may go.

Exit ALLEN.

And *vox populi*, my lord, is a very important voice indeed,
in this post-revolutionary age. My dear children: I am
dying. Will you set me in the sunshine.

They help him into a chair. He closes his eyes and droops his head.

Vox populi must be abided by. Lord Nelson, I want your
promise.

NELSON. And you have it, sir. Very solemnly.

He clasps HAMILTON's *hand.*

EMMA. He said he was dying?

NELSON (*quietly releasing the hand*).
          Yes: he did: and so he was.
          Among the sunflowers in his garden.

EMMA.
          I thought that he was going to sleep.

NELSON.
          No not asleep. He's dead. He said
          A word or two to wound me deep
          He said a word or two he never
          Said to you or me before.
          He said you were a whore.

EMMA.
          I am.

NELSON.
          You are my wife.

EMMA.
          Go on then, urge it urge it urge it –
          Beyond all possibility of belief!

FOR THE HEROINE: NOTHING:

Enter HARDY.

HARDY. I should have come in earlier, but I was told you had
   guests. A letter from the Admiralty, my lord. It has just
   this moment arrived.

NELSON (*tearing it open clumsily*). Admiralty – what – not
   now – no –

EMMA. The war?

NELSON. The war.

HARDY. The war. . . . This other letter, my lord, is personal –
   I had a certain delicacy about delivering it, but I suppose
   now –

NELSON (*opening it blindly and then suddenly realizing who it
   is from*). Hardy, you will be so good as to return this letter
   to the person who sent it – and will you write upon the
   cover: 'Opened by mistake by Lord Nelson, but not read. . . .'
   Napoleon is become Emperor: and I am the Mediterranean
   Commander-in-chief.

EMMA. And you are going to bring me with you?

NELSON. There is a child to be looked after. How can I bring
   you with me? Hardy – go back to London. Tell them I am
   ready. Be quick be quick be quick – the whole world is
   holding its breath!

HARDY. Aye aye sir.

Exit HARDY.

NELSON (*shouting*). Allen, where's my baggage – pack it up,
   get my uniforms, cabin-furniture, all my necessaries – we
   may be at sea for years – !

EMMA. You cannot just depart like this – in three minutes –
   and that's all.

NELSON. I have my orders in my hand and a black civilian
   coat upon my back – Good God, don't you understand,
   girl, I am neither a horse nor a herring at this moment –

Enter ALLEN *with the uniform.* NELSON *puts it on.*

Now once again we are in frame and return to our proper
element. Heaven help us but she's blubbering.

EMMA. Tom Tit would never blubber.

NELSON (*sings*).
    When Fanny bid goodbye to me
    She never shed one tear
    With her fingers she would pick the dust from my
        coat
    And straighten the curls of my hair.

EMMA (*sings*).
    When Emma bids goodbye to you
    Her great mouth is an open gutter
    Her eyes and her nostrils run in streams
    And she sweats like melting butter.
Oh God I can't see – oh Nelson, where are you, what are
you – how shall I remember you –

She kneels before him and feels him all over with her hands.
She sings.

    As a blind man knows his friends or his foes
    Through the memory of his touch
    So shall I know when you are gone
    What it is that I have lost.

ALLEN. Excuse me, milord – the old gentleman – do you
    think we should –

NELSON. I'll help you. Carefully . . .

He leaves EMMA *gently as she is still kneeling there with her*
eyes shut, and he and ALLEN *carry* HAMILTON *out.*
MRS CADOGAN *has entered.*

EMMA (*sings*).
    All through my life I chose the jewels and ornaments
    That on my body were the finest I could wear
    I had to begin when I was poor and ignorant
    With painted wooden beads and tinsel ribbons in my
        hair.

MRS CADOGAN. And crude though it was, there's no denying
she looked a treat.

EMMA (*sings*).

> But after a while I decked me out in silver filigree
>
> And delicate carved ivory as white as the new moon –
>
> – I walked with great precision and I tinkled with a
> music
>
> So elegant and rarified you could hardly hear the
> tune.

MRS CADOGAN. Of course – I said it wouldn't last . . .

EMMA (*sings*).

> But my legs they grew thick and my hips were like a
> brandy-cask
>
> I looked in the mirror and I saw it was no good –

MRS CADOGAN. . . . You see, poor Sir William what with
growing old and his illnesses and that, he didn't really
know how to appreciate her any more –

EMMA (*sings*).

> – So I hung myself with ironwork, with chains and
> hooks and cutlasses
>
> That swung so heavy on me that my haunches ran with
> blood.

MRS CADOGAN. But lovey, you must realize that Lord Nelson
was a hero and a very glamorous catch for a young woman
situated as you were: it's quite wicked to suggest it was
only a question of any old iron –

EMMA (*sings*).

> But now they're all discarded: I've cast them all away
> from me,
>
> They banged and clanged and rattled as I threw them
> on the ground:
>
> I'm poor and I'm ignorant: I'm just as you can see
> me –
>
> My hands are wide and warm and my breasts are
> large and round . . .

MRS CADOGAN. Of course they are, lovey.

EMMA. And that's all that there is.

MRS CADOGAN. Well, what more was there ever?

EMMA *suddenly becomes aware of her mother – whose remarks up till now have been no more than unobtrusive little whinings in the background.*

EMMA. I'm just left stupid. Fat, greedy, stupid: and the dirty bastard Frenchmen they've gone and they've taken all that was meant for *me*.

(*She sings.*)

> It's into them he will thrust his courage
> Till they toss their limbs and squeal –
> Oh sure he is worth his freestone pillar
> At the north end of Whitehall –

Four huge lions made of bronze and a great wide open square of nothing. That's for me: nothing.

Exit, with her mother uselessly hanging on.

TRAFALGAR – 1805:

Enter NISBET.

NISBET. And for me nothing neither. It is recognized that the Battle of Trafalgar saved England from invasion. It is recognized that after the battle Napoleon Bonaparte careered like a lunatic on the mainland of Europe from one ill-starred conquest to another till nobody but a lunatic could be sorry to see him go. And so we are all here: and *they* are over there, on the mainland of Europe: and that – one has always supposed – is how things ought to be ordered. As an enterprising and successful civilian merchant, I naturally had an interest in the situation remaining: *thus*. The French and Spanish fleets were caught up in Cadiz. Nelson was offshore. Admiral Villeneuve, in despair, for his career – he knew that Napoleon intended to replace him – finally decided to put to sea. I don't know what his battle-plan was. Nelson's was barbaric. But the whole thing was barbaric. That's why I'm not part of it. I was never any use as an officer anyway.

NELSON *gives his officers their orders.*

NELSON. I think you all understand what it is you have to do
this day. Bonaparte is not able to invade England without
a battle fleet to escort his army across the Channel. The
battle fleet lies in front of us and we are obliged to destroy it.
Destroy it absolutely. This can only be done by what I call
a pell-mell battle. We have no line to keep to, with each
captain geometrically selecting one enemy ship to lay himself alongside: instead we attack in two columns at right
angles to the French and Spaniards and we go straight into
the midst of their line – divide it into three portions – and
then create out of each portion a kind of whirling whirlpool –
a reckless expenditure – an accumulated crescendo of hap-
hazard destruction. Each of you, when you reach the middle
of it, will turn this way and that, you will each find your
enemy, you will hammer him and hammer him until you've
driven him under and then you will look around for the
next one. In effect then, there is no battle-plan once the
pell-mell has been set loose, and I intend to give no further
orders during the engagement. Each one of you is to do
exactly what you think best: and I think I have sufficient
experience of the abilities of you gentlemen to be quite
confident that it will work.

NISBET. He called this the 'Nelson touch' – it was like an
electric shock. Some shed tears, all of them approved. It
was new, it was singular, it was simple. Then he gave out
a signal:

NELSON. England confides that every man will do his duty.

NISBET. But they couldn't hang up 'confides' without using
too many flags so –

HARDY. So what about 'expects'. I suggest to you 'expects', my
lord, that entails no more than three flags.

NISBET. So with three flags it was done.

HARDY. Signal bent upon the halliards but not yet flown.

NISBET. Now then: two gentlemen who are to witness a
document. Oh the treacle, treacle molasses, spreading
treacle on an open wound –

NELSON (*taking two* CAPTAINS *aside*). I want you to witness
my will. I have a premonition of death.

NISBET. He had a premonition of death before the Nile and
before Copenhagen: I wish to God it would come true.

NELSON. I have added a codicil to the effect that I leave my
dear friend Lady Hamilton as a legacy to my King and
Country: for her eminent services towards which she has
as yet received no reward. Your signatures in witness, if
you please – (*To the audience.*) You are *all* to bear witness:
this is why you are here. It was written down and signed
by me: and signed by these two gentlemen: there is no
doubt of its legality.

Is it done? Then I thank you both: and so, back to your
ships. Now then, Captain Hardy, if you would have the
decks cleared for action?

HARDY. Clear the decks for action!

NISBET. The bulkheads are removed throughout the ship –
all tables and other non-essential articles are carried out of
the way. . . . The Bosun and his gang set to work to secure
the rigging and hang up nets to protect the decks from
splinters. . . . The Surgeon and his mates, in the lowest
level of the ship, prepare their make-shift operating theatre,
laying out seamen's chests for amputations and all the tools
that will be needed. . . . The gun-crews assemble their
gear and the balls of shot and cartridges are laid ready
behind each cannon. . . . To encourage the men who are
to die the band of the Royal Marines commences to play.

NELSON (*on his knees*). May the great God whom I worship –

NISBET. Blood and molasses, blood and molasses –

NELSON. Grant to my country, and for the benefit of Europe
in general a great and glorious victory. Amen.

NISBET. I know about blood and molasses – I do – was not
my own father a driver of slaves and a planter of sugar-
cane years ago in the West Indies?

The signal is now flown. Some officers cheer.

A SEAMAN. Do our duties – stands to reason: we're paid for
it, we're well-trained. But what the devil has England got

to do with it at this minute ? If we don't do our duty, the
Frogs'll do theirs and we'll be floating on the wavetops like
boiled mutton in a copper.

NISBET. *La France expectera que tous les hommes allons faire
leur devoir*. My French is very bad: but when Boney put
the same message on a bronze medal he had cast, I have no
doubt that every loyal Frog threw his hat in the air and
cheered.

HARDY. And all the stars upon his jacket make him an obvious
mark for sharpshooters. *I* don't propose to warn him: and
neither will anyone else: his temper is edgy enough this
morning as it is.

NELSON. Beat to quarters, Captain Hardy, if you please.

HARDY. Will you send the hands to quarters, if you please.

OFFICER. Bosun, send the hands to quarters! Drummer, beat
to quarters!

*Drum beats rhythm of 'Hearts of Oak' and the guns are got ready
in a sudden burst of physical action after the quiet of the last
minutes.*

OFFICERS (*at the guns*). Load ... Run out ... Prime ...
All guns ready for action, sir ... *etc.*

NISBET. Bear in mind the practical disadvantage of Lord
Nelson's plan of battle. As the British fleet in two columns
advances slowly towards the enemy, only the small guns
in the bows of the leading ships can fire. But the entire
larboard armament of the Frenchmen and Spaniards is
able to be brought to bear. Their roundshot and chainshot
whirl continually through our rigging: their canister-shot
ploughs among the sailors on our decks, time and again
and time and again and time and again: and the men must
endure it. They endure it for hours, so feeble is the wind
and so cunctatious is the slow encroachment of the fleet. ...
More blood and oozing sugar while they wait to be mutilated.

NELSON. Not much longer now ... Hardy: Lady Hamilton:
she must not be left destitute if I die.

HARDY. No sir. Very good, sir.

NELSON. I promised Sir William. *You* must promise *me*.

HARDY. I doubt if I shall have very much influence, my lord.

NELSON. You never approved of her.

HARDY. My lord, I never said so. I will do what I can. . . . We are nearly into 'em!

NELSON. Yes yes by God, any moment – where is a suitable gap ? Can we get through between those two ?

HARDY. No sir, it's too close – we'll have to run alongside one or the other.

NELSON. Then we'll take *him* – he's big enough, surely ? Into the gap, Hardy, quick!

HARDY. Let go lee-braces – lay sail aback – helm hard a-weather! And open fire all guns as soon as you can bear!

Fighting. NELSON *falls wounded.*

NELSON. Hardy, Hardy, quick. . . . They have done for me, Hardy, at last – my backbone is shot through.

HARDY. The Admiral's been hit – take him down to the cockpit.

NELSON. Put a scarf across my face and over the stars: the men must not know who it is has been hit. You come down below, Hardy, as soon as you can, and tell me how many ships we have taken: take at least twenty – I have bargained for twenty. I said look after Emma . . .

NELSON *is carried away.*

NISBET. When he died he asked Hardy to kiss him: and he did. I think he would have asked anyone to kiss him – except his own wife. He was buried in St Pauls.

THE HERO IS LAID TO REST:

The funeral procession: A CLERGYMAN *preaches.*

CLERGYMAN. To preserve our own liberty, Lord Nelson lost his life. It is only fitting therefore that upon his family and dependants we, a grateful nation, should bestow those intangible honours and material emoluments that he himself

would have received in person, had he been spared to do so.
Thus: by decision of Parliament, a pension of £5,000 per
annum is attached to the Nelson peerage, which devolves
upon the Rev. William Nelson, elder brother of the departed,
who also receives a grant of £10,000 to buy himself an
estate: £10,000 apiece to his sisters, and a pension of £2,000
per annum to Viscountess Nelson, widow of the departed –
of late unhappily estranged: but why should she not be
compensated? As for the other – ah – relict: and the alleged
unfortunate fruit of her companionship – we would do
better to think of her as one of those aberrations to which
genius is so often subject: and – bearing in mind the wounds
and frequent illnesses suffered by the late Lord Nelson –
let us draw a discreet veil, where it is impossible entirely
to condone: and let us above all not give her any money.
In the face of militant atheism, religious values, as of old,
reassert themselves in England. Lord Nelson was himself
the son of a clergyman. He would have wished it so.

THE HERO RISES UP:

NISBET. This is not to be construed as an historical recon-
   struction: and even as an act of poetic justice, I am afraid
   it will fall rather short.

He has lined up before him all the members of the cast (except for
EMMA *and* ALLEN) *who, in black cloaks have represented the
funeral party: and now he hands out fresh costumes – of a
pseudo-classical type, liberally spangled and be-tinselled –
together with plumed head-dresses. The general effect is reminis-
cent of one of the popular twopence-coloured prints of Nelson's
own period. The trappings of the funeral are quickly carried
away and a gilded marine-chariot (i.e. a vehicle shaped like a
sea-shell and drawn through the waves by tritons) is brought in
to replace them.*

NISBET.
   Caracciolo lost his life
   Old Hamilton could not keep his wife:

Equality, Fraternity, and so on never came:
And where we were then, now we are just the same.
This Hero fought for us 'gainst all the odds:
It did not help. So: now he's with the Gods.
We all are gathered here to send him off.
It would be better not to scoff.
We needed him: he did what we required:
He goes to heaven: that is his reward.
All of us, for whom he died,
Have no reward, because we never tried
To do without him on our own.
Here is a ship-shape chariot: let it be his throne.

NELSON *now arises from the bier. He is in his uniform with perhaps a bright patch of red to mark his fatal wound. He mounts into the chariot with* FANNY *on one side of him.* EMMA *now enters and joins him there on his other side. The Fourth Actress, attired as a* MERMAID (*or, if this is inconvenient, a* SEA-NYMPH) *arranges herself in front of the chariot. If there are more than four ladies in the cast the number of Mermaids can be increased accordingly. The rest of the players group themselves in a baroque composition around the chariot.*

NELSON (*sings*).
        The hero rises up to reach
        His everlasting proud reward.
        Here his true lovers, each and each,
        By him are equally adored.
EMMA AND LADY NELSON (*singing*).
        No more hatred, no jealousy nor fear,
        Nelson's Paradise is here.
NELSON. This is, of course not possible. . . . But what more
    can a sailor want?
EMMA (*sings – the refrain in this song sung by all the ladies*).
        With our hero now we shall arise –
        (With a fa la la la la la)
LADY NELSON (*sings*).
        He'll gaze for ever in our eyes –
        (With a fa la la la la la)

MERMAID (*sings*).
>For what the world may think or say –

EMMA (*sings*).
>We damn the world –

LADY NELSON (*sings*).
>>We lie and play

ALL LADIES (*singing*).
>We are for ever flown away
>(With a fa lal lal la la la la la la
>With a fa lal lal la la la la . . .)

NELSON. So stand by to haul away!

ALLEN (*still dressed in his usual costume*) *enters briskly.*

ALLEN. Stand by to haul away!

NELSON. Mr Allen, you are still wearing your working clothes
   – how is that ? Find yourself an ornament at once – or –

*His voice falters and a tremor of disturbance runs through the
cast as if they are suddenly conscious of their own artificiality.
Then* NELSON *pulls himself together.*

   I know! You are promoted Bosun. That make you happy ?

ALLEN *is expressionless.*

   Yes of course it does. So haul away!

ALLEN. Hands to the halliards! Wait for the whistle. Hand-
   somely now – remember: we've got ladies aboard. Haul!

*The Bosun's whistle is blown and there is a noise of ropes being
hauled and the rhythmical cries of seamen. The cast all sing the
'Fa la la' song once more – in unison – and the chariot rises up
with its three passengers. (If it is not possible to fly it an effect of
downwards-moving lights may help to simulate rising).*

Appendix

This play is a long one. The authors would prefer it not to be cut: but if it proves impossible to present it in its entirety, the scene in Act Three headed 'A Bird upon a Perch' may be omitted and replaced by the following shorter episode:

YOUR WHORE AND HER BAD BREATH:

Enter HAMILTON *in a dressing-gown, looking frantic.*

HAMILTON. Please leave my house. You are making far too much noise and have continued to do so for seventeen days. Lady Hamilton has borne with you in patience and so has Lord Nelson: but I am not at all well and I would be glad if you would go.

EMMA. He's quite right. He is not well. I think you had better go.

NELSON *makes a helpless gesture.*

RELATIVES. Well, really, whose house is it? I mean, who is married to whom? We never had this sort of nonsense when we used to go and stay with Fanny – Fanny knew how to entertain her guests – after all we're not just anybody, we are the family, Goddammit . . . *etc.*

The RELATIVES *retire, grumbling – the old clergyman singing gaily in his wheelchair.*

HAMILTON. I am dying . . .
　　　　You are left, upon my death,
　　　　With your whore and her bad breath.
　　　　What will she do, tomorrow?
　　　　Will she steal, or will she borrow?
　　　　Or else, will you, with your great reputation –

NELSON.
    Demand her upkeep from a grateful nation!
HAMILTON.
    You take the words out of my mouth.
NELSON.
    I know what I am about.
    The services which she has wrought
    For love of me, for all this land,
    By all this land with open hand
    Shall be rewarded in abundant measure!
    I will inform the people: they will pour out their
    treasure.
HAMILTON. They will: they must: by heaven you must
promise me they shall! Mr Allen!

Enter ALLEN.

    How many wives is a sailor expected to have?
ALLEN. A wife in every port, sir?
HAMILTON. Exactly so. *Vox populi*. You may go.

Exit ALLEN.

    Vox populi, my lord, is a very important voice indeed, in
this post-revolutionary age. *Vox populi* must be abided by.

He dies.

EMMA. He said he was dying?
NELSON.
    Yes: he did: and so he was.
    Among the sunflowers in his garden.
EMMA.
    He looked as though he was falling asleep.
NELSON.
    No not asleep. He's dead. He said
    A word or two to wound me deep
    He said a word or two he never
    Said to you or me before.
    He said you were a whore.
EMMA. I am.

NELSON. You are my wife.

EMMA.

>   Go on then, urge it urge it urge it –
>   Beyond all possibility of belief!

NB: *If this shorter scene is preferred, of course there will be no need for* MRS CADOGAN *to drop the child's toy in the earlier part of the Act.*

Methuen's Modern Plays

EDITED BY JOHN CULLEN

Paul Ableman	GREEN JULIA
Jean Anouilh	ANTIGONE
	BECKET
	POOR BITOS
	RING ROUND THE MOON
	THE LARK
	THE REHEARSAL
	THE FIGHTING COCK
John Arden	SERJEANT MUSGRAVE'S DANCE
	THE WORKHOUSE DONKEY
	ARMSTRONG'S LAST GOODNIGHT
	LEFT-HANDED LIBERTY
	SOLDIER, SOLDIER and other plays
John Arden and	THE BUSINESS OF GOOD
Margaretta D'Arcy	GOVERNMENT
	THE ROYAL PARDON
Brendan Behan	THE QUARE FELLOW
	THE HOSTAGE
Edward Bond	SAVED
	NARROW ROAD TO THE DEEP NORTH
John Bowen	LITTLE BOXES
Bertolt Brecht	MOTHER COURAGE
	THE CAUCASIAN CHALK CIRCLE
	THE GOOD PERSON OF SZECHWAN
	THE LIFE OF GALILEO
Shelagh Delaney	A TASTE OF HONEY
	THE LION IN LOVE
Max Frisch	THE FIRE RAISERS
	ANDORRA
Jean Giraudoux	TIGER AT THE GATES
	DUEL OF ANGELS

Rolf Hochhuth	THE REPRESENTATIVE
Heinar Kipphardt	IN THE MATTER OF J. ROBERT OPPENHEIMER
Jakov Lind	THE SILVER FOXES ARE DEAD and other plays
Henry Livings	KELLY'S EYE and other plays
	EH ?
John Mortimer	TWO STARS FOR COMFORT
	THE JUDGE
Joe Orton	LOOT
	CRIMES OF PASSION
Harold Pinter	THE BIRTHDAY PARTY
	THE ROOM and THE DUMB WAITER
	THE CARETAKER
	A SLIGHT ACHE and other plays
	THE COLLECTION and THE LOVER
	THE HOMECOMING
	TEA PARTY and other plays
Jean-Paul Sartre	CRIME PASSIONNEL
Theatre Workshop and Charles Chilton	OH WHAT A LOVELY WAR

Methuen's Theatre Classics

THE TROJAN WOMEN
Euripides
*an English version by
Neil Curry*

THE REDEMPTION
*adapted by Gordon Honeycombe
from five cycles of Mystery
Plays*

THE MISANTHROPE
Molière
translated by Richard Wilbur

IRONHAND
Goethe
adapted by John Arden

DANTON'S DEATH
Buechner
*an English version by
James Maxwell*

THE GOVERNMENT
  INSPECTOR
Gogol
*an English version by Edward
O. Marsh and Jeremy Brooks*

BRAND
Ibsen

THE WILD DUCK
translated by Michael Meyer

HEDDA GABLER

THE MASTER BUILDER

MISS JULIE
Strindberg
translated by Michael Meyer

LADY WINDERMERE'S FAN
Wilde

THE IMPORTANCE OF
  BEING EARNEST

THE UBU PLAYS
Jarry
*translated by Cyril Connolly
and Simon Watson Taylor*

THE PLAYBOY OF THE
  WESTERN WORLD
Synge

Methuen Playscripts

Paul Ableman	TESTS
	BLUE COMEDY
Barry Bermange	NATHAN AND TABILETH and
	OLDENBERG
Kenneth H. Brown	THE BRIG
David Campton	LITTLE BROTHER: LITTLE SISTER
	and OUT OF THE FLYING PAN
Henry Chapman	YOU WON'T ALWAYS BE ON TOP
David Cregan	THREE MEN FOR COLVERTON
	TRANSCENDING and THE DANCERS
Harrison, Melfi,	NEW SHORT PLAYS
Howard	
Henry Livings	GOOD GRIEF!
John McGrath	EVENTS WHILE GUARDING THE
	BOFORS GUN
David Mercer	THE GOVERNOR'S LADY
Georges Michel	THE SUNDAY WALK
Rodney Milgate	A REFINED LOOK AT EXISTENCE
Guillaume Oyono-	THREE SUITORS: ONE HUSBAND
Mbia	and UNTIL FURTHER NOTICE
David Selbourne	THE PLAY OF WILLIAM COOPER
	AND EDMUND DEW-NEVETT
Lanford Wilson	HOME FREE! and THE MADNESS OF
	LADY BRIGHT

Other Plays from Methuen

Jean Anouilh
: COLLECTED PLAYS VOLUME I
(The Ermine, Thieves' Carnival, Restless Heart, Traveller Without Luggage, Dinner with the Family)
COLLECTED PLAYS VOLUME II
(Time Remembered, Point of Departure, Antigone, Romeo and Jeannette, Medea)

Bertolt Brecht
: PLAYS VOLUME I
(The Caucasian Chalk Circle, The Threepenny Opera, The Trial of Lucullus, The Life of Galileo)
PLAYS VOLUME II
(Mother Courage, St Joan of the Stockyards, The Good Person of Szechwan)

Max Frisch
: THREE PLAYS
(The Fire Raisers, Count Oederland, Andorra)

Jean Giraudoux
: PLAYS VOLUME I
(Tiger at the Gates, Duel of Angels, Judith)
PLAYS VOLUME II
(Amphitryon, Intermezzo, Ondine)

John Millington Synge
: PLAYS AND POEMS